NICHOLAS ROYLE is the author of five short story collections – *Mortality, Ornithology, The Dummy and Other Uncanny Stories, London Gothic* and *Manchester Uncanny* – and seven novels, most recently *First Novel.* He has edited more than two dozen anthologies and is series editor of *Best British Short Stories* for Salt, who also published his *White Spines: Confessions of a Book Collector.* Forthcoming is another collection, *Paris Fantastique* (Confingo Publishing). In 2009 he founded Nightjar Press, which continues to publish original short stories as limited-edition chapbooks.

SHADOW LINES

*Searching for the Book
Beyond the Shelf*

NICHOLAS ROYLE

SALT

SHEFFIELD

PUBLISHED BY SALT PUBLISHING 2024

2 4 6 8 10 9 7 5 3 1

The Joel Lane part of the chapter 'Three reminiscences' was read at
a symposium on Joel Lane and his work, 'The Witnesses Are Here',
at Voce Books, Birmingham, on 11 November 2023, organised by
Clive Judd with support from Gary Budden of Influx Press. The
first part of the chapter 'Mike Nelson's books' first appeared in the
autumn 2022 issue of *Swedenborg Review*. Thank you to the editors,
Stephen McNeilly, James Wilson and guest editor Gareth Evans.

First published in Great Britain in 2024 by

Salt Publishing Ltd

18 Churchill Road, Sheffield, s10 1fg United Kingdom

www.saltpublishing.com

Salt Publishing Limited Reg. No. 5293401

A CIP catalogue record for this book is available from the British Library

isbn 978 1 78463 307 3 (Paperback edition)
isbn 978 1 78463 308 0 (Electronic edition)

Typeset in Granjon by Salt Publishing

Printed and bound in Great Britain by Clays Ltd, Elcograf S.p.A

For Gareth Evans

'I love you more than words can tell.'
Unsigned note found inside Bret Easton Ellis's *American Psycho* bought from Oxfam Books & Music Islington, 1 October 2023

Contents

Introduction   1

Reginald the Surrealist Engine   13
Walking and reading   32
The numbers   59
Unread books   74
Getting off at Stoke   91
Books in films   122
Three reminiscences   152
Mike Nelson's books   167
Home again, home again   177
Project For a Walk in New York   194

Acknowledgements   223

Introduction

I said to my publisher that I wanted to do a follow-up to *White Spines*. He said, Sure, go ahead, but make sure it doesn't feel too much like a follow-up. Sequels never do as well.

I thought of *The Godfather Part II* and *Terminator 2: Judgment Day*. I thought of *Paddington 2*. I didn't think of *Aliens*, because *Aliens* is a vastly inferior film to *Alien*, and you are free to disagree, but I'm not going to change my mind. Even *Alien³* is better than *Aliens* and *Alien³* is not very good.

I am aware that this is a book, not a film.

White Spines had a narrative: the edge-of-your-seat story of my quest to collect all the white-spined Picadors published by that publisher between 1972 and 2000, when they abandoned the classy look that had been more or less a guarantee of quality.

This book, *Shadow Lines*, would be different. It would make a virtue of not having a narrative. It wasn't that I couldn't think of one. I toyed with various exciting plotlines – the hunt for all the white-spined King Penguin paperbacks published between 1981 and 1987; the quest to collect all the white-spined Paladin paperbacks published between 1986 and 1992; the search for all the white-spined Sceptre paperbacks published between 1986 and 1994 – and rejected them all. I do collect those books, as well as the white-spined paperbacks of Abacus and Vintage and Black Swan, but I wanted the new book to be more than a find-and-replace job.

I wanted to write about my collection of the Rev W Awdry's Railway Series stories, and, more to the point, about the illustrations. Everyone, I imagine, who has any interest in Thomas the Tank Engine and friends, has their own favourite illustrator. I wanted to write about mine – C Reginald Dalby – and the connections I started to see between his work and the paintings of the great Belgian surrealist René Magritte.

I wanted to write about the *Penguin Modern Stories* series of anthologies from the late 1960s and early 1970s edited by Judith Burnley, not to be confused, despite the fact that in my head I do it all the time, with author Julia Blackburn. I will try not to do it in this book.

I wanted to write more about what I call 'inclusions' – ephemera found within the pages of second-hand books, like insects in amber, which are known as inclusions – and how they have become often more important to me, in my collecting, than the authors, titles or printed contents of many books. I wanted to write about how I find them, by means of what I call 'shadow lines'. I wanted to write about books in which people have scribbled phone numbers. I wanted to write about books in films and books in the work of installation artist Mike Nelson.

I wanted to write about walking and reading, about people I see doing it and the books they are reading, and about my own decades-long compulsion to do it, too, and about the books I am reading when I am doing it.

I realised I was acquiring – and keeping in my home – books that perhaps ought to be in other homes. I wanted to write about some writers I have known who have died. I wanted to vent about one or two things. I wanted to write about a cult classic that I first read in the late 1980s and see if I still think it's the masterpiece I thought it was then. I also wanted to share some more of my overheard conversations in bookshops and dreams about books. These will be dropped in here and there.

The search for the white-spined B-format Picador paperbacks published between 1972 and 2000, which provided the main focus of *White Spines,* is ongoing.

Visiting family in Shrewsbury on a Saturday in July 2021, I went for the first time to Welsh Bridge Books & Collectables, an excellent shop that sprawls over three floors of a very old building – 'MIND YOUR HEAD' – with an interesting selection of books. One section is devoted to Beat writers. There were titles by Kerouac and Burroughs and, to my great delight, a Picador I hadn't known existed, *Kentucky Ham*, by William Burroughs Junior, marked 'RARE' and costing only £2. I'm not even sure I'd known that William Burroughs Junior existed.

I'm not sure either how after that I ended up in Erotic Literature, but it was there that I found Trevor Hoyle's *The Hard Game* (New English Library). I'm a fan of the string of novels Hoyle published with John Calder – *Vail*, *The Man Who Travelled on Motorways* and *Blind Needle* – which might be characterised as experimental or speculative. (*Blind Needle* was the first book I was commissioned to review for the *Guardian*, although the review never appeared.) Wikipedia describes Hoyle as a science fiction author; *The Hard Game* appears to add yet another string to his bow.

After we had exhausted Welsh Bridge Books & Collectables, my wife's brother-in-law took me to the lovely Raven

Bookshop in Shrewsbury's Market Hall, where I added Elizabeth Hardwick's *Sleepless Nights* to my collection of Virago Modern Classics, and a Raven Bookshop badge to my collection of button badges. Finding Candle Lane Books closed, we called in at the Oxfam Bookshop, where I found Rilke's *The Notebooks of Malte Laurids Brigge* (Picador Classics) and Ben Lerner's *The Hatred of Poetry* (Fitzcarraldo Editions). Hatred is a strong word, but I didn't enjoy Lerner's first two novels, *Leaving the Atocha Station* and *10:04*, enough to make me want to read his third, *The Topeka School*. As for this slim volume of non-fiction, I was curious to find out if I would like Lerner more if he turned out to hate poetry (despite being a poet and a poetry editor).

I have now read *The Hatred of Poetry* and couldn't actually tell you what is Lerner's opinion of poetry.

I found three new-to-me Picadors in one place in Carlisle. Anyone who knows their second-hand bookshops will know specifically where in Carlisle.

Where else but Bookcase? I'd gone there – to the bookshop's café, Cakes & Ale – to meet artist and Picador cover illustrator Paul Leith and as a bonus he had brought along his lovely wife Tina. We had coffee and rainbow cake, and found we had a few acquaintances in common, such as Paul's fellow book cover artist John Holmes (who I never actually knew, but I had been in contact with his family over the proposed use of two of his images) and artist and figurative painter Andrew Ratcliffe (who had been my art teacher at school). In the shop I found three books with covers by John Holmes – Ivy Compton-Burnett's *A Heritage and Its History*, Vladimir Nabokov's *Quartet*, and *Possible Tomorrows* edited by Geoff Conklin – and three Picadors not among my collection – Stacy Schiff's *Véra (Mrs Vladimir Nabokov)*,

Tony Parker's *The People of Providence* and Ajay Sahgal's *Pool*. I picked out another Picador, Italo Calvino's *Cosmicomics*, with a cover by the Brothers Quay, previously owned by a Bernard Fison. It struck me as an unusual name; I looked him up.

A retired stockbroker, Bernard Fison sailed his yacht around the world, before returning to his family's holiday home in the Cumbrian village of Boot and subsequently making Boot his permanent home. Singing in a local choir, taking art classes and becoming a church warden, he lived village life to the full, while at the same time raising money for the poor of Sri Lanka, where he had been shown great kindness on his round-the-world trip.

In 2007, he was involved in a serious four-vehicle accident on the A595 and died at the scene, leaving a son, two daughters, a brother and a granddaughter.

Now, thanks to Bookcase, I have his copy of *Cosmicomics* – and his 1000 lire note, bearing a picture of another world traveller, Marco Polo, which I found tucked inside at page 59. In a coincidence that Calvino would perhaps have enjoyed, the only other Italian currency I have found in a second-hand book was also a 1000 lire note, also with Marco Polo, in a 1987 Paladin edition of *The Wine-Dark Sea*, a 1973 short story collection by Calvino's contemporary, Leonardo Sciascia, with a striking cover by the great James Marsh. The banknote in *The Wine-Dark Sea* had been inserted at page 61.

In October 2018 a new second-hand bookshop, Yum Yum, opened in Tib Street, in Manchester's so-called Northern Quarter. I failed to write about it in *White Spines*, although I thought that I had. At some point over the next two years, it changed its name to Anywhere Out of the World. The last time I saw Louis, the young man who dared to open a bookshop when more people were closing bookshops than opening them, he was sitting barefoot on his couch in the middle of the shop declaring that he was retreating from the world of the senses into a world of interiority. Since then, however, the business has expanded. Expect great things.

Talking of great expectations, I was in upstairs in Richard Booth's Bookshop in Hay-on-Wye on Wednesday 4 August 2021 when I became aware of a hubbub at the far end of the room. I heard the end of a brief speech, an announcement, a burst of applause. I gathered that a young couple had just become engaged. He talked about having pinched a ring so that he would be able to order the correct size of engagement ring. She said something about the bookshop. It seemed that maybe they were connected with the shop in some way. Perhaps they had worked there, or perhaps still did. I hope they enjoy a long and happy life together.

Amid the excitement I found some good books, at Hay prices, some of them. Marguerite Duras's *Le ravissement de Lol V Stein* (Folio) with the name of a previous owner, Damien Bertrand (*juin* 1988), and an inclusion, a business card from a restaurant, Michel Chabran in Pont de l'Isère. Another French book, Monique Wittig's *Virgile, Non* (Editions de Minuit), withdrawn from the library of the University of Sheffield. A Sceptre first novel, *Watercolour Sky*, by William Rivière, two novels by Anita Mason – *The Racket* (Sceptre) and *The War Against Chaos* (Abacus) – and a Picador with a horrible brown-speckled white spine, Tama Janowitz's *American Dad*, which I will try to replace with a non-speckled spine. It looks like they were aiming for rag-roll and got bog roll instead.

On an honesty shelf in an alleyway I found *The Picador Book of Modern Indian Literature* edited by Amit Chaudhuri, published in 2001 but with the old white spine. This was very exciting for me, because previously the latest iterations of the white spine I had seen, and bought, had been from 2000.

A week or so earlier, I had been to Sharston Books, in south Manchester, for what I thought would be my last visit. Novelist and short story writer Neil Campbell was still working there, but he was on notice; by now the shop was closed to customers and open for online orders only. Neil let me in. Among many other interesting finds I came across another Marguerite Duras, in translation (by Barbara Bray), *Blue Eyes, Black Hair* (Flamingo), a copy previously owned by ex-Factory Records boss and Manchester impresario Tony Wilson, who had used the inside back cover to write out a ten-point plan of action. Point one was 'Create new entity'. Point four, 'All rights transferred to the new entity' etc.

In fact, Sharston Books limped on into 2022. On Sunday 29 May 2022, I saw on Facebook, at 1pm, that Sharston Books would be open that day, for the last time, until 2.30pm, so I walked down to the river, over Simon's Bridge, around the golf course, down the various paths and arrived to find the gates locked, and a woman indicating that I should go around to another entrance. A sad sight awaited me. Most shelves cleared. Classics gone. A young man behind the desk playing on his phone. Upstairs, miles of empty shelves. In the shipping container devoted to fiction I picked out ten for a tenner, including one with a good shadow line.

When you are looking down on the top edge of a book block – the pages of a book that have been glued or stitched together to form a single unit – and you see a line of shadow that suggests that within lies treasure, be it a train ticket from London to Tiverton Parkway dated 12 April 2001 inside E Croxford's copy of Ruth Brandon's *Surreal Lives* or a birthday card from Anita to Bernard in Dashiell Hammett's *The Dain Curse* in which Anita has written, 'The first of many together', that line, that parting of pages, is what I call a shadow line.

Daphne Merkin's *Enchantment* (Paladin) had a strong shadow line near the end of the book – page 241, I saw, when I removed it from the shelf and opened it and found a little stash of nine children's drawings. If the former owner of this book were ever to read this and want them back, nothing would give me greater pleasure than to return them. The same goes for any inclusions that I describe in this book.

Although I write somewhere in these pages about how finding books that you are missing from a collection out in the wild is more exciting than being given them, the generosity of friends and strangers who have given me Picadors, and other books, must be acknowledged. I have experienced the pleasure of giving, and the pleasure of receiving should begin with an appreciation of the act of giving. So, thank you to David Batt, without whose offer of two Picadors he knew I didn't have – Richard Klein's *Cigarettes Are Sublime* and Joe Queenan's *Imperial Caddy* – I would almost certainly never have entered the doors of Brooks's Club, St James's, where I went to pick them up. On the way there I had called in at the Skoob Books pop-up in the Brunswick Centre where I had found another Richard Klein title, *Eat Fat*, which had also eluded me up to that point. And on the way to Skoob, I had popped into Oxfam Books & Music Islington and spotted the faintest of shadow lines on the top edge of a Livre de Poche edition of Amélie Nothomb's 2010 novel *Life Form*, revealing a to-do list that I hope it is not too indiscreet to reproduce here:

> Card for Penny
> ~~LSO sing-in = book~~
> ~~Food for lunch/Sonia~~

Plan Sun lunch
~~email Bridget~~
Letter – Zara (re pyjamas)
~~Hackney vouchers~~
~~email Carla/Billy~~
email Gill
~~write Sally~~
~~Phone scaffolding~~
French h/work
CQ to bank
Band

Impressively efficient – I have no doubt that Sunday lunch was eventually planned, but I'd love an update on 'Letter – Zara (re pyjamas)' and I hope the author of the list had more luck with Zara than I did with Uniqlo when trying to exchange an item with a receipt but without the price tag (which incorporates a computer chip).

I have lost count of the number of Picadors given to me by Gareth Evans. On a Saturday in October, 2021, he gave me a copy of *The Dispossessed* by Robert McLiam Wilson and Donovan Wylie. The same day, I had been, with my wife, to Brighton and we had visited the Smallest Bookshop in Brighton, which on that day took the form of a stall on Brighton Open Market. Proprietor John Shire had emailed after reading *White Spines* to say he had a copy of *The Freud/Jung Letters* edited by William McGuire and abridged by Alan McGlashan that he would put aside for me. My wife picked out Mary McCarthy's *The Groves of Academe* (Panther) and I also selected a first edition of *Frights* (Gollancz) edited by Kirby McCauley. When *Frights* went into paperback it was divided into two volumes and I only have the first one, which doesn't include Robert Aickman's story, 'Compulsory Games', or for that matter stories by Ramsey Campbell and Dennis Etchison. *Frights* and Mary McCarthy, along with *The Freud/Jung Letters*, came to £14, but John sold them to me for a tenner. That's my kind of second-hand bookseller.

Two people each gave me a copy of Gilbert Sorrentino's *Mulligan Stew*, both expressing surprise that I hadn't already got a copy, but due to what I can only call a cock-up on the record-keeping front, I can't say who either of these people was.

Sometimes, although not very often, I see a book I would like to buy – for its inclusion or inscription, perhaps – but don't.

At 5pm on a Saturday afternoon in December, 2022, I was making my way through the crowds in Portobello Road when I spotted a book stall on the market. I had a look. Lots of stock, including Picadors and ghost story anthologies from the 1960s and '70s. I picked up a Picador and quickly put it down again – £10 for a Picador? Don't make me larf. I picked up *The Fourth Fontana Book of Great Ghost Stories* edited by Robert Aickman. I collected this series years ago – alongside the *Fontana Book of Great Horror Stories* and *Pan Book of Horror Stories* series – and had always been missing one volume, the fourteenth, until I found it in Oxfam in Durham in June 2022 for a couple of quid. Pencilled on the flyleaf of this copy of the fourth volume was the price: £25. Twenty-five big ones? Cor blimey, strike a light, guvnor! Talk about ripping off the tourists. More interesting to me was what was written in green ink on the inside front cover. 'A present from my brother. This book belongs to Melanie Boycott.' I took a picture, glowered my intense disapproval towards the stall generally and melted back into the crowd.

I found a Melanie Boycott on Etsy and sent her the picture

I had taken of the book and a short message. Later, Melanie replied by email. She was the same Melanie Boycott; it had been her book. 'I've travelled around a bit, since I owned it,' she wrote. I explained that had it been a couple of quid, I would have bought it and sent it to her, but that it was ridiculously overpriced. 'My brother would have got me that when we lived in Barnsley,' she continued. 'It was a time you all had to have a fountain pen for school and I had a bottle of green and a bottle of purple ink.' I, too, used green ink in my school exercise books, green and turquoise.

Melanie went on: 'We then moved to Tywyn in Gwynedd and from there I went to Sheffield Polytechnic. After staying in Sheffield for a while I moved to Skipton where my mum and dad had a caravan.'

By now, if things have gone according to plan, Melanie should have moved to Earby in Lancashire, but historically part of Yorkshire. Her son, she told me, lives in London, but otherwise she has no connection with the capital. Apart from that outrageously overpriced copy of a book her brother gave her.

In August 2021, in Oxfam Books & Music Islington, I found a lovely Penguin Modern Classics edition of Flann O'Brien's *At Swim-Two-Birds* with a wraparound cover that reproduces *The Bus by the River* by Jack B Yeats. On the inside front cover in distinctive, almost Gothic, handwriting, in purple ink, is the name Penny Ashbrook, followed by 'Manchester 1973'. On the facing page, the flyleaf, in tiny handwriting in the top-left-hand corner, close to where, sadly, the jacket is starting to come away from the book block, we read, '8 for £1.'

At page 141 there is an inclusion, a theatre ticket designed to look like an old £1 note. 'From Edinburgh,' it says, 'At Swim-

Two-Birds. Christ's Theatre. 8.30pm Oct 16th–20th.' The price given is 35p.

Only in November 2023 does it occur to me to ask novelist and short story writer John Ashbrook, who I know, and whose partner Elizabeth Baines I also know, because they live near me in Manchester, whether Penny Ashbrook might be any relation. In fact, I ask Elizabeth, and she tells me that Penny is John's daughter and, although she lives in New Zealand, she is staying with them at the moment. In 1973, Penny was in Cambridge, but was coming and going between Cambridge and Manchester. After that she lived in north London before moving to New Zealand in 2004, where she works as a TV writer, director and producer.

Frustratingly, in November 2023, I can't find my copy of the book and was working from my notes relating to its purchase in 2021. I find it on a wet and windy night in January 2024, the night before I am due to deliver the manuscript of this book (the latest – and definitely the last – in a series of deadlines). There's no reason why Penny should want the book back – she gave it away, after all – but it might be fun to see it again, and if she has returned to New Zealand, maybe John would like to see it. He can either keep it or give it back to me.

I slip the book into a padded envelope and head out into the night.

Reginald the Surrealist Engine

In the first episode of the new era of *University Challenge*, presented by Amol Rajan and broadcast on 12 July 2023, the new question-master asks the team from Trinity College Cambridge the following bonus question: 'A murderer at the scene of his crime and two bowler-hatted men armed with a club and a net feature in which painter's 1927 Surrealist work *The Menaced Assassin?*' It's the detail of the bowler hats that allows the Trinity team to answer, with confidence, 'Magritte.'

Three years and one fortnight earlier, on 27 June 2020, just days after non-essential shops were allowed to reopen following the first national Coronavirus lockdown, I came off the M6 at Coventry, parking on Brighton Street in Upper Stoke. Or is it Barras Heath, or perhaps Ball Hill? I don't know, but the key thing was I was at least a mile from the centre of Coventry and parking was unrestricted. Plus, there was a good stretch of road with back gardens on one side and a high privet hedge on the other: I could park without inconveniencing anyone. Indeed, no one was actually parked here. There didn't appear to be anyone around at all. I walked down towards Walsgrave Road, a high brick wall having appeared on my right to shield local residents from the noise of the traffic on Jimmy Hill Way. At Gosford Green I turned right and walked along Far Gosford Street, heading towards the Big Comfy Bookshop and hoping it would be open. I had done my research, which suggested it was supposed to be, but in June 2020 we were all more used to seeing shops closed than open.

It was open and it turned out to be a good bookshop to visit immediately post-lockdown, because it had a generous amount of floor space – concrete, painted red, if you want to know. There were even armchairs, also red, but they were taped off. 'CAUTION,' shouted the yellow plastic tape. 'ATTENTION.' My eye was caught by a more welcoming, handwritten sign affixed to a shelf of old books. 'OLD BOOKS,' it said. 'Is there any better smell than that of old books? Come and browse for a while, you never know what you might find.' I found a novel, in hardback, *The Exhibitionist*, by Henry Sutton. I could see that it couldn't possibly be by my contemporary Henry Sutton, author of *The Househunter* and *Flying* and numerous other novels, unless he had been a child prodigy and written it when he was four. I decided to buy it and write to Sutton and ask him if he knew about it, maybe offer to send it to him if he was interested, and was about to head with it to the till when on a low shelf I spotted a short, slim black spine, title in white, Bodoni Ultra bold italic – that wasn't the title, that was the typeface. The title was *Toby the Tram Engine*. Or:

TOBY THE TRAM ENGINE

If you can imagine that white out of black.
In fact you don't need to.

TOBY THE TRAM ENGINE

I read it while walking back to the car. *Toby the Tram Engine* is number seven in the Railway Series of books by the Rev W Awdry, first published in 1952, but the reprints I collect are from the 1960s and '70s, as they remind me so strongly of my childhood. I love everything – well, almost everything – about them, from the typeface on the spine and front cover, to the small format, the very fact of their being a numbered series, and of course the stories themselves. But, most of all, I love the illustrations, which, as I hope to show, are not just engines with pretty faces, but evidence that the ambition of one of the Railway Series artists extended way beyond the island of Sodor.

There was tension and conflict on the railway, however, and not everything ran smoothly.

The first book in the series, *The Three Railway Engines*, was first published in 1945. Awdry had written three stories for his young son, Christopher, and, with his wife's encouragement, had submitted them to publisher Edmund Ward in 1943. A fourth story was requested and this set the template for *The Three Railway Engines* and the next twenty-five books in the series, all written by Awdry, the last of these, number twenty-six, appearing in 1972. Eleven years later, Christopher Awdry took up his pen and added a further sixteen books to the series.

The first edition of *The Three Railway Engines* was illustrated by William Middleton. Awdry was unhappy with Middleton's work and it's easy to see why – the features sit rather flatly and sketchily on the moon-like faces of the engines – and he was replaced for the second book, *Thomas the Tank Engine*, by Reginald Payne, whose style was livelier and more vivid, the faces more expressive. Sadly, however, Payne suffered a nervous breakdown and was himself replaced for book three, *James the Red Engine*, by C Reginald Dalby, who also redid Middleton's illustrations for later editions of *The Three Railway Engines* and made a number of alterations to Payne's work on *Thomas the Tank Engine* – Thomas backs into a station instead of facing forwards; extra luggage appears on a platform; telegraph poles and a signal gantry are added to countryside scenes; a water tower gets a different pipe; and a van changes colour from green to brown – although my edition, dating from 1969, does not credit either illustrator.

Dalby would remain the series' illustrator until (and including) book eleven, *Percy the Small Engine*, in spite of Awdry's increasing dissatisfaction with his work as well. The author complained that Dalby's illustrations were inaccurate and inconsistent. When we see, for example, in *Tank Engine Thomas Again*, Henry standing at a platform, still in his blue livery that he had been given at the end of the first book, but with square buffers and two side windows in his cab, instead of round buffers and one side window, in other words looking exactly like Gordon, who is also blue, it is hard to disagree with Awdry. There was further inconsistency in Henry's wheel arrangement: originally drawn as a 4-6-0 locomotive, he would sometimes appear as a 4-6-2 engine. Don't worry if you don't know what these mean; trust me, it's an inconsistency.

When Awdry described Percy, in the eleventh book, *Percy the Small Engine*, as resembling 'a green caterpillar with red stripes', Dalby, a successful commercial artist and the creator of the famous Fox's Glacier Mints polar bear logo, packed up his brushes and refused to illustrate any more Railway Series books, citing late delivery of scripts as the reason why.

'I was sorry to give up,' Dalby is quoted as saying, or writing, in a video posted on YouTube by ClickClackTrack. 'I had become intimately involved with my engines, their characters and personalities; but, like that other famous "artist" Adolf Hitler, my patience became exhausted.'

If Dalby did say, or write this, you have to think it's an unwise and somewhat baffling comparison to make, but when I look at the raised right arm of the vicar in the final illustration in *Percy the Small Engine*, I wonder if he was playing a long game. He certainly seems to have found Awdry – who, let's not forget, was a reverend – pedantic and difficult to work with, while the relationship between the two men might have been doomed from the start. When original *Thomas the Tank Engine* illustrator Reginald Payne had gone AWOL, Awdry had done some sketches of his own for book three, in collaboration with his friend Barbara Bean, but when he sent these to editor Eric Marriott, the answer came back that an artist, Dalby, had already been engaged. One can imagine even a cleric's nose might have been put out of joint.

Dalby was replaced by John T Kenney, whose colours were a little less bright, most noticeably in the green livery worn by Percy, Henry and Duck, but who enjoyed a good working relationship with Awdry and was only replaced after book seventeen, *Gallant Old Engine*, when his eyesight began to fail. For book eighteen, *Stepney the 'Bluebell' Engine*, the commission went to Swedish artist Gunvor Edwards, who asked her husband Peter to assist her and they shared the illustration credit until book twenty-six, *Tramway Engines*, which was Awdry's last. Their style was more impressionistic; to me, the faces look all wrong, perhaps because the first faces I had seen had been Dalby's and so those, to me, were the originals, the real faces, imprinted on my mind, and any that came later were inauthentic, unconvincing, poor substitutes.

For similar reasons, perhaps, actual trains today seem to me more like plastic toys than real trains. Which is not to say I miss the days of steam; I had to go out of my way, to the Keighley and Worth Valley Railway, for example, to encounter steam, or happen to be on York station when *Sir Nigel Gresley* called by with a special. The trains that moved me were the AM4 electric multiple units I would travel on as a boy from Altrincham to Manchester Piccadilly; the Class 25 diesel locomotives and Class 40s and occasional Type 3s and Brush 2s that I would see pulling goods trains through Skelton Junction; the Peaks I would cop, or even cab, at Piccadilly as they stood waiting to pull the Harwich Boat Train; the Class 76 electric locos I would goggle at, at Guide Bridge, with their widely spaced window eyes and diamond-shaped pantographs (yes, I was a trainspotter, in case you hadn't guessed). These were, and remain, *real* trains, because they were the trains I encountered at an impressionable age, when my mind was like the grey putty in Magritte's painting *The Reckless Sleeper*, which may not be a perfect analogy, because the grey 'tablet', as the Tate website calls it, in the Belgian Surrealist's 1928 work, probably represents the sleeping mind, but the way those symbolic 'everyday objects' – mirror, bird, bowler hat, bow, candle and apple – are 'embedded' in it suggests to me an act of imprinting.

Today's trains, while they might get me where I'm going in a shorter time, don't seem altogether real and an after-effect of lockdown, once we were permitted to travel again, was to put more people back in their cars and fewer on trains.

On 22 September 2020 I was driving up the M1. I left the motorway at junction 14 and skirted Newport Pagnell, parking a mile out of Olney and walking back in to visit the Oxfam Books & Music. It was quite a small shop and I found nothing I wanted until I spotted a battered copy of *The Time Out Book of Paris Short Stories* (Penguin). I edited this anthology for Time Out, but have few copies, so I thought I'd buy it rather than leave empty handed. Plus, it had an inclusion, but one of the least interesting ones I'm sure I will ever find, a tiny scrap of brown envelope with sealing gum on one side, tucked in at page 45, the first page of Toby Litt's 'Story to Be Translated From English into French and Then Translated Back (Without Reference to the Original)'. Whatever music had been playing over the Olney shop's music system switched to Van Morrison. Following his recent pronouncements on the subject of Covid 19, I thought I could do without Van Morrison, so left, walked back to the car and drove north, heading for Market Harborough. Again, I parked out of town and walked back in, again, to visit the Oxfam Books & Music. It somehow didn't feel, as Olney hadn't, that it would prove to be a treasure trove on a level with Harpenden, say, or St Albans or the fabled Berkhamsted shop. All I found was *Edward the Blue Engine*, book nine in the series, so one of those illustrated by C Reginald Dalby. Again, I read it as I walked back to the car.

Readers may know that Thomas the Tank Engine and his friends inhabit the fictitious island of Sodor located between the Isle of Man and mainland Britain. Wilbert Awdry was born in Romsey, Hampshire, in 1911. His father was Vicar of Ampfield and many of his parishioners were railwaymen. He would visit them, at the station and at their platelayers' huts beside the railway, and sometimes he would take his son along. In 1917 the Awdry family moved to Box. It is said that the young Wilbert would lie awake in bed at night listening to trains effort-fully climbing the hill to Box tunnel and he would imagine that they were talking to themselves. '"Can I do it? Can I do it? . . .

Yes, I can. Yes, I can."' Awdry, a lifelong railway enthusiast and keen railway modeller, would later say that most of the stories in his Railway Series were based on real events. And some of the characters were based on real people, too. In the story 'Saved From Scrap', in *Edward the Blue Engine*, a traction engine called Trevor is heading for the scrapyard before a kindly vicar steps in to save him. Could this be a case of the author writing a flattering version of himself into the series? Apparently not, since Awdry appears in later books as the Thin Clergyman, accompanied by the Fat Clergyman, who was based on his friend, the Rev Teddy Boston, a fellow railway enthusiast and owner of a traction engine called *Fiery Elias*.

Wednesday 5 October 2022
Oxfam, Kendal.
Female customer: Ooh look at that! Isn't that cute? Kids' books
   are always better, because they've got pictures in. Our books
   should have pictures in. Adult books should have pictures in.
Male customer: Hm.
[...]
Her: Have you seen that one that's collectable? *Footsteps in the
   Snow* or summat. You should look out for that. It's valuable.
Male customer: Hm.

If you like visiting second-hand bookshops and you haven't been to Astley Book Farm, well, what are you doing tomorrow?

   On Monday 20 June 2022, I was in the car on the M1 again, this time accompanied by novelist, Small Pleasures podcast creator and (at that point, although not for much longer) Manchester Writing School colleague Livi Michael. Driving north, we slipped on to the M6, then came off at junction 3 for Astley Book Farm, which is just a couple of miles north of the motorway, but, with its miles of bookshelves, thousands of books, and café boasting the largest fondant fancies I've ever eaten, a world away.

Livi had been recommending Ruth Rendell, so I picked up her Arena Novella, *Heartstones,* to join my small collection of Arena Novellas. I also found a duplicate copy of the Penguin edition of Derek Marlowe's *The Disappearance*, one of my favourite novels of all time, and a lovely Penguin Modern Classics edition of Raymond Radiguet's *Devil in the Flesh*. To replace my C-format edition of Stephanie Merritt's *Gaveston* (Faber), I picked up a B-format mass-market edition from the same publisher. (In a bid to relieve congestion, I am replacing hardbacks with paperbacks, and C-format paperbacks with B-formats.) Livi kindly bought me a copy of *Paris Tales* (Oxford) edited by Helen Constantine.

We had coffee and fondant fancies then drove on to Lichfield, where, in the Oxfam Books & Music I found a lovely clean B-format edition of Tom Fletcher's *Witch Bottle* (Jo Fletcher Books) to replace my C-format and Helen Hodgman's *Blue Skies & Jack and Jill* (Virago Modern Classics) for its wonderful cover, *Night and Day* (1938), by the British Surrealist Roland Penrose. Livi was drawn to a copy of Paul Auster's *The New York Trilogy* in the crime section, which made me realise I should always check the crime shelves when looking for copies of *The New York Trilogy*. Luckily this copy was lacking any interesting elements, so I bought it for her, which might sound a bit odd until you've read the chapter in this book on *The New York Trilogy*, 'Project For a Walk in New York'.

We then went a couple of doors down to the St Giles Hospice bookshop, where, because we didn't have a bag between us, we showed the manager the books we'd bought in Oxfam and she teased us for having gone there first. I responded that we'd saved the best till last. Then, however, I didn't find anything and was about to buy two CDs of Greig's piano music, out of desperation, when I spotted a stack of Railway Series books, so I bought all seven.

At home, from my purchases I picked out *Henry the Green Engine*, illustrated by Dalby, and settled down with a brew. I nearly spat out my tea when I got to the penultimate page of the last story, 'Henry's Sneeze'. Henry is determined to punish some naughty boys who have been dropping stones from a bridge and have broken some of the windows in Henry's coaches. His intention is to teach them a lesson by 'sneezing' when he next goes under the same bridge: 'Smoke and steam and ashes spouted from his funnel. They went all over the bridge, and all over the boys who ran away black as n—.'

When complaints were made in 1972, twenty-one years after the volume's original publication, Awdry at first stood his ground, arguing oversensitivity on the part of the race relations board, but later apologised and changed the description to 'black as soot'. In my edition, a reprint from 1974, the N-word is still present. (In a second edition dating from 1952 that I saw in Oxfam Bookshop Wanstead, in October 2023, the N-word had been crossed out in ballpoint pen and the word 'soot' added.)

Luckily, there are more positive things to talk about in *Henry the Green Engine*. Such as the advertisements in the form of posters on the station wall in the penultimate illustration in the first story, 'Coal'. Henry stands at the platform smiling in the direction of the Fat Controller while on the wall behind him we can see two posters. One reads: 'You must read "THE THREE RAILWAY ENGINES"' and the second one says, 'READ ABOUT "JAMES THE RED ENGINE"'. Later in the same book, in the penultimate story, 'Percy and the Trousers', a double-decker bus going over a bridge has a banner advert on its side reading 'TROUBLESOME ENGINES'. This was the second time the creators of the series had indulged in playful subliminal advertising. In the first story, 'Thomas and the Guard', in *Tank Engine Thomas Again*, Thomas is pulling coaches Annie and Clarabel out of a station, while in the foreground the station bookstall has a poster on its exterior wall reading, 'NOW IN STOCK JAMES THE RED ENGINE', and a newspaper headline board next to it headed 'GRAND NEWS' and, printed underneath, 'ALL ABOUT THOMAS THE FAMOUS TANK ENGINE'.

This metatextual device, even while calling attention to itself as artifice and to the fictionality of the Sodor universe, has the unexpected effect of making the world of the story more believable. *Look! They're advertising the world of the books within the world of the books!* It shouldn't work and yet it does. Was this Awdry's idea, or Dalby's, or perhaps that of the editor, Eric Marriott? My money is on Dalby. Awdry had a bee in his bonnet about Dalby's shortcomings, but Dalby's mind was on the bigger picture. Awdry may have been the showrunner, as it were, with the island of Sodor forever expanding like a huge model railway inside his head, but Dalby was the art director or production designer, creatively inserting allusions here, visual quotations there.

It was *Toby the Tram Engine* that opened my eyes to Dalby's ambition. In the final story in that book, 'Mrs Kyndley's Christmas', the second illustration shows Mrs Kyndley sitting up in bed in a red dressing-gown waving to Toby, who is passing along the line immediately outside her bedroom window. On the wall to the right of the window is a framed picture of Toby in exactly the same kind of landscape as he appears in outside Mrs Kyndley's window. Not only that, but in both images, Toby-outside-the-window and Toby-in-the-picture-in-the-frame-on-the-wall, the tram engine is sporting a new bright-blue horizontal band just above his red buffer bar, which was promised him in the previous story by the Fat Controller. On the wall to the left of the window is a similar framed picture showing Thomas in what appears to be the same location. This mise en abyme has an effect similar to that of the advertisements for other books appearing in earlier books discussed above, but also subtly different. Toby has only just had that blue element added to his livery and yet Mrs Kyndley, a kindly woman who happens to live right next to the railway line, has already got a picture on her wall of Toby with the blue band. Are we to believe she is a railway enthusiast, with a particular interest in the Fat Controller's railway, or is there some unspoken connection between her and, say, the Fat Controller? Has the Fat Controller snuck in and put those pictures on her wall? Or are we simply happy that the so-called 'Author', who addresses the reader in brief introductions at the start of each of the books, has engineered the mise en abyme? Again, my money is on Dalby.

The second story in *Toby the Tram Engine*, 'Thomas in Trouble', features, to begin with, not Toby, but Thomas. The tank engine is fetching some trucks back from the quarry and encounters a policeman, in fact a 'large policeman', who is startled by Thomas and out of spite, perhaps, upbraids Thomas for not having a cow-catcher attached to his front. The fifth illustration switches location from the line where the altercation takes place to the morning room or dining room of the Fat Controller, where that gentleman is sitting having breakfast while his wife is standing at the window and the butler has entered the room to inform him that he is wanted on the telephone, which we can see off to the right through the open door into the hall. As I was reading this book on my walk back from the Big Comfy Bookshop to my car parked on Brighton Street in Coventry, I looked twice at this illustration. There was something about it, some nagging familiarity, beyond the possibility that I had seen it before as a child. There was something about the combination of different elements that resonated with me.

I have loved the paintings of Magritte almost as long as I have been a fan of the Railway Series. The first Magritte I ever saw, thanks to Andrew Ratcliffe, my art teacher at school whose portrait of Prince Charles, which once hung in the National Portrait Gallery and now belongs to the King, was *The Empire of Light* (1954), subtle and beguiling with its night-time neighbourhood and daylight sky, but my favourite is probably *The Menaced Assassin* (1926). I wrote a short story about it, 'The Cellar', published in *Four For Fear* (PS Publishing) in 2012 and reprinted in *The Dummy and Other Uncanny Stories* (Swan River Press), little suspecting that a decade later I would find myself attempting to argue that *The Menaced Assassin* is a model for the fifth illustration in the second story in *Toby the Tram Engine*.

In *The Menaced Assassin*, a man stands in a room listening to a gramophone. Beside him, his hat and coat are draped on a chair and his suitcase stands alongside, while behind him the body of a woman with blood on her face lies on a red couch. Behind her is a window through which we can see mountains in the background and, immediately outside the window, the heads of three men looking into the room. In the foreground of the painting, two men in bowler hats, one on either side of the picture, lie in wait outside the entrance to the main part of the room to apprehend the murderer. One, on the left, carries a club, the other a net.

In both paintings – the Magritte and the Dalby – there is a room in the foreground/middle ground and a window in the background. In both cases the view out of the window is of an unpopulated landscape, with mountains or hills on the horizon. In both cases, in the left middle ground there is a woman. In the Magritte there is the body of the murdered female; in the Dalby, the Fat Controller's wife stands on a red carpet holding one of the drawn curtains, as if she has just finished opening it. The Fat Controller sits at the breakfast table in the middle of the room, side on to the window, but he has turned away from it to face the butler, who has entered the room, so he, the Fat Controller, has his back to the window, just as Magritte's murderer has also. The Fat Controller and the murderer are located in the same spot in each painting, each facing in the same direction. The butler stands in the same spot as the man with the net, from where he is explaining to the Fat Controller that there is a telephone call. Although we can see the actual telephone on a table in the hall, through an open doorway on the right, the *idea* of the telephone hangs in the air between the Fat Controller and the butler, in the same location as that of the gramophone – near-homophones that are not unlike each other in some respects, each bringing forth sounds from another place. The telephone call is to inform the Fat Controller of the fact that Thomas is in trouble with the police, just as it seems reasonable to assume that the bowler-hatted men in the Magritte are police, tooled up to apprehend a murderer.

Of course, there are differences. The Fat Controller is not a murderer, but nevertheless he will have to deal with the police.

The Fat Controller's wife is, thankfully, alive, but could the fact she is standing at the window looking out suggest she might long for another life, rather than one in which she brings her husband more coffee, as the text informs us, while he fills his stomach at a breakfast table laid for one? The murderer has done a terrible thing, yet seems unconcerned as he listens to music on the gramophone before attempting to leave the scene of the crime. The Fat Controller has been enjoying breakfast, another sensory experience, before he will have to encounter the police. There is no equivalent figure, in the Dalby, of the man with the club, although we may think of the two men as a single unit. There are no watchers at the Fat Controller's window, but the Fat Controller already feels seen. No train moves on his railway, notwithstanding the fascinating semi-autonomy of the engines themselves (for instance, Henry's refusal to leave a tunnel in which he is sheltering from the rain, in 'The Sad Story of Henry' in *The Three Railway Engines*), without his say-so.

But why would Dalby choose to base his humble illustration on a famous painting by Magritte? What's the point? Is it a one-off? Is there any other evidence of his interest in fine art? Well, yes, arguably.

The mise en abyme that we see later in *Toby the Tram Engine*, already discussed, is a familiar device in art, being employed in works by artists from Jan van Eyck to Dorothea Tanning. Dalby seems to have a particular interest in the Surrealists. It's hard to look at certain of his illustrations and not be reminded of the steam locomotives in the background of numerous works by Giorgio di Chirico, such as *The Joy and Enigmas of a Strange Hour*, *Ariadne's Afternoon* and *The Soothsayer's Recompense* (all 1913). The penultimate illustration in 'Tenders and Turntables', the second story in *Troublesome Engines*, in which James spins round and round on the turntable, has something of Marcel Duchamp's *Nude Descending a Staircase, No.2* (1912) about it, while on the very next spread, Dalby's illustration of James, Gordon and Henry attending an 'indignation meeting' in their shed at night shows light pouring through the side windows and skylights despite the fact that the moon is no fuller than a crescent. Magritte illustrated a similar impossibility in *God's Salon* (1948), in which a large house surrounded by mature trees is bathed in apparent sunshine despite the sky being of deepest, darkest blue studded with stars and a crescent moon.

One of Awdry's criticisms of Dalby's work focused on his inconsistency with scale or perspective. Sure, maybe, in 'Thomas in Trouble', the policeman is too small in relation to Thomas when we see them both in the first illustration, or too big in relation to Thomas in the second illustration. Or, maybe, Dalby had seen Magritte's *The Giantess* (1929–1930), featuring a small man and a large woman (in scale with the room around them), and couldn't get it out of his mind.

Trains were an important subject for another Belgian artist associated with Surrealism, Paul Delvaux, but his most notable railway paintings, such as *Suburb* (1956) and *Evening Train* (1957), in both of which we see a familiar trick of the light, in this case using insulators on telegraph poles to reflect more light than could possibly be shed by a crescent moon, came after the publication of *Troublesome Engines*. Locomotives were not absent from Magritte's work: *The Nightingale* (1962), in which a steam engine speeds away from a town under a pink sky whose only cloud offers a resting place for a god-like figure, postdates Dalby. *Time Transfixed* (1938) will be familiar to anyone who has ever bought the Penguin Modern Classics edition of Edward Upward's *The Railway Accident* for its cover alone. An engine of a type not dissimilar to Gordon or Henry emerges from a fireplace under a marble mantelpiece on which stand a clock, and two candlesticks, only one of which is reflected in the mirror above. The time on the clock is a couple of minutes before a quarter to one. The painting could have been in Dalby's mind when he painted any of his engines leaving the darkness of a tunnel, but I'm not pushing that anywhere near as hard as the similarities between *The Menaced Assassin* and the Fat Controller at Breakfast.

The time on the station clock in the third illustration in the story 'Duck Takes Charge' in *Percy the Small Engine*, Dalby's swansong, says just gone twenty-five past six. (We know from the text that this is in the evening.) This picture reminds us not of Magritte or any other Surrealist or even a painter, but of Hal Morey's celebrated 1930 photograph of light falling through the semi-circular windows of Grand Central Station. The window at the end of Dalby's station interior has a very similar construction to those in Morey's photograph. Deliberately? Maybe. A criticism that Awdry made of Dalby was that he would not get out and look at engines in the real world and use these as the basis for his drawings. Dalby admitted as much, but we should perhaps not assume that this was because he couldn't be bothered. I think he had seen Morey's photograph and Magritte's paintings, and Di Chirico's, and for that matter those of Edvard Munch (the final illustration in 'Mrs Kyndley's Christmas', of carol singers outside Mrs Kyndley's house, bears more than a passing resemblance to two paintings by the Norwegian: *Red Virginia Creeper* and *The Village Street*), and wanted to pay tribute to them or simply absorbed elements of existing works and allowed them to be expressed in his own illustrations. Magritte, though, would appear to be the artist to whom he most frequently and most obviously paid homage. We should not be surprised. One of Magritte's most famous works is *Not to Be Reproduced* (1937), a portrait of an English poet and patron of the arts showing the back of his head as he stands before a mirror, and, in the mirror, the back of his head again. The name of the subject? Edward James. When I look at that picture I see the back of Edward James's head and the back of Edward James's head reproduced in the mirror (although according to the rules of physics, of course, it shouldn't be), but I also see two of Awdry's engines, Edward and James, either on separate platforms at Edward's station in 'Old Iron' in *Edward the Blue Engine*, or coupled together in 'James and the Top-Hat' in *James the Red Engine*. That story, 'James and the Top-Hat', contains seven illustrations. Two of them show James on his own, and, of the five that show James and Edward together, four of those show Edward on the left and James on the right, meaning that if we scan from left to right, as I tend to do and I believe many others do too, we 'read' 'Edward James', and in the one illustration that shows Edward on the right and James on the left, the two engines are coupled together with Edward in front and James behind, so really we're still seeing 'Edward James' even in that case. And if you picture one engine-with-a-face lined up behind and coupled up to another engine-with-a-face, it's kind of like Magritte's painting of Edward James looking into a mirror and seeing the back of his own head. (As for Henry James, see chapter 'Books in films'.)

Why not have a look for yourself if you still need convincing? There's an excellent Thomas the Tank Engine Wiki that has galleries for each book, allowing you to scroll through all the illustrations, story by story, and Magritte's paintings are easily found online. *The Menaced Assassin* is, as the time of writing, on view in the Museum of Modern Art in New York.

2

Walking and reading

On 24 April 2022, I walked from Stoke Newington to Crouch End reading Jonas Karlsson's *The Room*, a short, fascinating novel about a man who finds a room at his place of work that no one else will acknowledge exists. Karlsson is a Swede and writes, not unreasonably, in Swedish, but I had found a French edition the day before in Oxfam Books & Music Islington, translated by Rémi Cassaigne and published by Actes Sud, in a narrow-format edition of 190 pages. It's a strange experience reading a novel translated into a language other than your own. I now think of *The Room* as a French novel, even though I know it's not. Indeed, I would have referred to it here as *La pièce* but for the fact that a quick check online revealed to me that it has indeed been published in English translation. Hogarth published a hardback edition translated by Neil Smith, which ran to 176 pages, and an omnibus appeared in paperback from Vintage in 2019, combining *The Room* with *The Invoice* and *The Circus*. The blurb describes the three texts as novellas, despite the fact the Hogarth edition of *The Room* was billed as a short novel. I try not to get too worked up about this sort of thing, but I remember very clearly being advised at school, by my German teacher, Mr Arthur Shutt, that a novella was not just a short novel, but a distinct form characterised by certain restrictions: restricted numbers of characters, plotlines, locations et cetera. Nothing to do with the number of words or pages. We were studying Thomas Mann's *Tonio Kröger*; I wished we could have been studying Mann's *Death in Venice* instead.

Mr Shutt maybe didn't realise, although I'm sure he might have suspected, that some of us were reading *Tonio Kröger* not in German, but in the Penguin Modern Classics translation by HT Lowe-Porter. I was never very good at German, so I don't know why I later chose to read it alongside French at university, as even at that level I would try to find all my set texts in English translation. The only one I couldn't find, for some reason, was Goethe's *The Sorrows of Young Werther*, but my lecturers allowed me to drop Goethe and do Schiller instead, who, while I may not have been able to find him in translation, wrote in simpler German and the texts were clearly legible, whereas, somewhat unbelievably, the only German text of *The Sorrows of Young Werther* available at that time was in Gothic script.

Finding myself unable to concentrate at home, in my shared flat in Archway, or in the university library, I got into the habit of reading while walking around north London. I did most of my finals revision completing circuits of Highgate Cemetery. After leaving education, I continued to read while walking. I remember reading a Panther edition of JG Ballard's collection *The Overloaded Man* while walking south down Hornsey Road when it started to rain. It was the southern part of Hornsey Road – largely residential, no pubs – so no opportunity to try the Fraser McIlwraith Method.

I had been introduced to Fraser McIlwraith by Andrea Wedekind during my first week living in Paris as a student on my year abroad. Andrea was a friend of Philippe Gras, alongside whom I had worked as a waiter at Pizza on the Park in the summer of 1984. I slept on Andrea's floor for my first week in Paris and at the weekend she hosted a party and introduced me to Fraser and it was on his floor in rue St Martin in the 3rd arrondissement that I slept for the next month, before I found a studio flat to rent in the 19th. Some years later, I met Fraser in London and as we were walking in Mayfair, it started to rain quite heavily. Follow me, said Fraser, as he entered Brown's Hotel on Albemarle Street, where, I should perhaps point out, he was not staying. At reception he asked if a black collapsible umbrella had been handed in. One was produced, Fraser said thank you, and we exited on to Dover Street.

I have acquired a number of umbrellas over the years, using the Fraser McIlwraith Method. I much prefer it to carrying one that might not be required.

In today's throwaway society, if I'm caught in a downpour, I simply reach for the first abandoned umbrella I see. Yes, they may have the odd broken spoke, but they're usually good enough to see you through a sharp shower, and once it's stopped raining, you can drop it in the nearest bin or leave it in a convenient spot for someone else to pick up.

On Hornsey Road, with JG Ballard's *The Overloaded Man*, in the rain, there were no umbrellas to hand, but the book had a broken spine and was falling apart, so I decided it didn't matter if I read it in the rain. Indeed, I remember dropping each detached page, once read, into a rubbish bin as I passed one.

I recently found myself with a looseleaf copy of Doris Lessing's collection *The Story of a Non-Marrying Man and Other Stories*, picked out of a pavement box of free books in Brixton for me by my daughter. She chose it for the (broken) spine, being familiar with my collection of orange-spined Penguins (particularly the orange spine with author's name in black and title in white). Although I already had a copy, of the same edition, I gladly accepted this one, despite its poor condition, (a) because it was offered by my daughter and (b) because it would be handy to read in the rain. I read it walking around Manchester, in the rain, and you might imagine, therefore, that I got through it in a day or two, but my pride in my northern roots makes me want to tell you that it doesn't actually rain in Manchester as much as you might think, although August 2023 was pretty wet everywhere and I did get through it in a day or two.

We have moved on since the 1980s and, as I completed each soaking page of the Doris Lessing, I sought a bin with recycling options.

I found it a rather uneven collection with some rather pedestrian stories, which you might think would suit the reader-walker, and some stand-outs, such as 'An Old Woman and Her Cat', in the reading of which I was interested to find I cared more about the fate of the cat than that of its owner. Forgive the spoiler, but the old woman dies first and it's the death of the cat that is contiguous with the end of the story. Given that I am not one of those people like the woman I overheard on a mobile phone yesterday saying 'I hate people. I can't stand people. I can't bear humans. Keep me away from humans', I was puzzled by this, until it occurred to me that maybe the very structure of a story can affect – or indeed prompt – emotional responses. Maybe I was more affected by the death of the cat because, as I followed that thread of the narrative, I knew the end of the story was approaching? Is it instinctive to become emotional around endings, in narrative as in life?

In another story, 'Out of the Fountain', Lessing writes about rape in a way that's similar to how some male authors wrote about it at the time: 'A man who wants a woman will rape her, if she is around, or rape another in her stead if she is not. Women get raped; and those who want to be will make sure they are where the raping is.' Should we think less of Lessing for this, as we might of male writers who come up with similar remarks, in the 1960s and '70s? Or does it give us more context against which to consider those remarks?

I liked the unusual form of 'An Unopened Love Letter'; it made me sit up and take notice and read more carefully, although trying to sit up while walking led to my doing my back in and needing a lie-down. The longest story, 'The Temptation of Jack Orkney', starts brilliantly and then goes on a bit, which I find that longer stories so often tend to do. We call them short stories for a reason.

To return to Crouch End, in the excellent Oxfam Books & Music there I bought three old copies of *Fantasy & Science Fiction* magazine from a shelf full of them, March 1984 for 'End of Season' by Tina Rath, February 1989 for 'The Demonstration' by Marc Laidlaw and March 1982 for an inclusion, at the first page, a card from the London Zoological Society with, on the other side, a note to self or a note to the cobbler: 'Reheel red boots with super strong and durable heels. To be ready on Thursday'. Maybe, actually, it's a note from the cobbler to him or herself. Excellent short stories all three, if I include the cobbler's note. Still in Crouch End, my wife joined me in Flashback Records, where I was buying too many Morton Feldman albums, and together we went to Waterstone's to look at their red-spined Vintage Classics paperbacks.

A few days earlier I had been walking from my flat in Didsbury into Manchester reading Rosanna Hildyard's mini collection of stories, *Slaughter* (Broken Sleep Books), and had got only as far as Withington, when I passed another reader-walker, a young woman in shorts and a sleeveless top carrying a backpack. She was reading a paperback with a thick red spine, the distinctive red of Vintage Classics. The Vintage Classics design positions, or used to position, the word 'Vintage' where you might reasonably expect to see the author's first name, so that you ask yourself, who is Vintage Bennett, who is Vintage Brontë, who is Vintage Murakami? And once you've worked out that there isn't anybody called Vintage Murakami, you ask yourself, how would Ryu Murakami feel, if he came across 'Vintage Murakami' and asked himself, which of my books is this? Is it *Almost Transparent Blue*? Is it *Coin Locker Babies*? Is it *In the Miso Soup*? But it's none of those, because it's actually a book by Haruki Murakami, by only a couple of years the older of the author Murakamis and by far the more famous. I was going to add that I find Haruki less interesting than Ryu, but recognised that that would be essentially a random observation prompted solely by a coincidence of nomenclature. It's not a competition. But then the design quirk of the Vintage Classics list turns it into one.

What would you think if you came upon a book declaring itself to be 'Vintage Bennett'? Would you think Alan Bennett? Or Arnold Bennett? And what about 'Vintage Brontë'? There are actually two Brontës in the Vintage Classics list: *Wuthering Heights* by Emily Brontë and *Jane Eyre* by Charlotte Brontë, assuming that's not actually *Charlotte Brontë* by Jane Eyre, as I often joke to my wife. The evenings fly by.

There's a Vintage Grossman – *Everything Flows* by Vasily Grossman – and a David Grossman, whose *More Than I Love My Life* is published by Vintage, but not in their Classics list. Or not yet.

I could go on.

I know, I already am doing.

I got a look at the cover of the book the young woman in Withington was reading, but not a good look. I formed an impression of red and black type in a large point size and that was about it. Enough to recognise it if I were to see it again, but not enough to describe it to someone who might be able to identify it. When I got into town I dropped into Waterstone's on Deansgate and checked out the Vintage Classics, but couldn't find a cover that looked like the one I'd glimpsed in Withington. In London at the weekend, I inspected the Vintage Classics in Waterstone's Islington Green – no luck – but on the Sunday in Crouch End, in the Waterstone's that tries a little bit too hard to look like it's not a Waterstone's, a bookseller offered assistance. I told her what I was looking for and the search caught her imagination and she had a good old look for it and found it in non-fiction, where I had not thought to look. The book was Solzhenitsyn's *The Gulag Archipelago*. The bookseller, Lena, was a credit to her trade.

As my wife and I walked back to Stoke Newington, we saw a man in his forties walking down Green Lanes wearing a navy jacket over a down gilet, black jeans and white trainers, and reading a thick paperback that he was holding in his right hand. Unfortunately he had the front cover folded over the back cover so that I couldn't see what he was reading. Not enough of the back cover was visible even to begin to attempt identification.

Saturday 23 April 2022
Oxfam Books & Music Islington.
Two tall, middle-aged, male customers, one bald, one with

tattoos on face and neck. Tattooed Man, browsing literature shelves, picks out Joseph Conrad novel and shows it to Bald Man.
Bald Man: There's a joylessness about him that I can't bear, a
  heaviness.

After Anna Burns won the Man Booker Prize in 2018 for *Milkman*, a novel set in an unnamed city at an unspecified time but clearly about the Troubles in Northern Ireland, more than one person (two, actually) told me I should read it. For some reason (as I get older I find I am increasingly put off by long novels, and most people would say it's not even that long, at 348 pages), it took me five years to get around to it, but now that I've read it, I can see why they thought I should.

The unnamed narrator of *Milkman*, known as 'middle sister', tells us on page three that a car drew up alongside her while she was 'walking along reading *Ivanhoe*'. She goes on to tell us, 'Often I would walk along reading books. I didn't see anything wrong with this but it became something else to be added as further proof against me. "Reading-while-walking" was definitely on the list.'

The man who speaks to her from the driver's seat invites her to hop in, but, as she tells us, she didn't want to get in the car with him. Still, she felt she didn't want to be rude as he hadn't been rude towards her. So, she simply explains to him that she is walking, and reading. 'I held up the book, as if *Ivanhoe* should explain the walking, the necessity for walking.' He tells her she can read in the car, which is not a great argument, since it's well known that reading in cars can make you feel sick.

Often, when I'm walking down the high street, I will use the fact that I am reading as an excuse for not engaging with chuggers or survey takers or religious maniacs. In some cases they choose not to interrupt my reading, and in other cases they do interrupt and I motion to the book and say, 'I'm working,' which in some cases is kind of true, like when I was reading *Milkman*, since I was only really reading it for research.

Two pages later, the milkman approaches the narrator again. She tells us: 'I was alone and not reading this time, for I never read while running.' Very wise. I have not even attempted to read while running, or, you may be relieved to learn, while driving. If I'm not reading while walking, I'm likely, while walking, to be trying to work out a problem in my writing, since that is something else that, increasingly, I find I can't do sitting down, even with a notebook or a laptop. In fact, especially with a notebook or a laptop. Nor can I do it, which I know some people can, while driving a car, or swimming, or, to come back to *Milkman*, running.

On page 58 of *Milkman*, one of the narrator's brothers-in-law warns her of the dangers of reading-while-walking, which he describes as 'unsafe' and he says amounts to 'cutting off consciousness' and 'not paying attention and ignoring your surroundings'. This just goes to show that the brother-in-law doesn't know what he's talking about. People do ask me if I walk into lampposts (no) or step in dog dirt (no) or bump into other people (again, no). It's not like I literally have my nose in the book – peripheral vision allows me to see obstacles and avoid them – and nor is it the case that I never look up. I look up often and if the person coming towards me has their eyes on their mobile phone it's invariably me who moves to one side. If the person coming towards me makes eye contact, I will be receptive and will happily exchange a nod or a smile, and this is the thing: I have noticed lots of smiles. It is definitely the case that people I pass in the street are more likely to smile if I have just looked up from a book. And more likely to start a conversation. And, if it isn't about direct debits or my shopping habits or the word of God, I'm always happy to reciprocate. Actually, if they do want to talk about God, I have a quick look at *their* literature and if they are Jehovah's Witnesses I mutter the words 'child killers' and keep walking.

Well, that's what I *want* to do and *think* about doing, and if you don't know why, may I recommend Ian McEwan's novel *The Children Act*, which I read while walking around Hackney in July 2022?

The narrator of *Milkman*, however, appears to agree with the brother-in-law regarding reading-while-walking being isolating, since two pages later she says, 'I knew that by reading while I walked I was losing touch in a crucial sense with communal up-to-dateness . . .' She goes on to acknowledge that knowledge of what was going on didn't prevent things from happening. 'Purposely not wanting to know therefore, was exactly what my reading-while-walking was about. It was a vigilance not to be vigilant . . .' (I wish there were a comma before 'therefore' as well as after, but there isn't.)

My own vigilance with regard to responsible use of the shared pavement or path is constant – or I hope it is – which is why I was so aggrieved at the man in Canon Aly.

Canon Aly is a narrow north-south alley in the City of London connecting Queen's Head Passage to St Paul's Cathedral. I don't know why it's called Canon Aly or even if 'Aly' is derived from 'alley'. Tom Cruise pops up there in *Mission: Impossible – Fallout* (2018) and Channel Four's *First Dates* used to be filmed in a restaurant just around the corner. On Sunday 19 March 2023, the day before my birthday, I was walking from Stoke Newington down to Tate Modern in search of Yves Klein postcards. I was reading a Picador edition of Flann O'Brien's *The Third Policeman*, having somehow made it to very nearly 60 without ever having read Flann O'Brien. I know. It's scarcely believable.

Heading south through Canon Aly towards St Paul's, I become aware of a couple in front of me and slightly to the left, who suddenly turn right, directly across my path, as I continue walking straight on. We don't collide, but it could go down as a near miss. The man, wearing a red puffer jacket and carrying an M&S plastic bag, says, 'Reading and walking. *Tch.*'

I say, 'What's wrong with reading and walking?'

He says, 'You can't see where you're going.'

I say, 'You turned right. I was walking in a straight line.'

He says, 'Oh, shut up.'

I say, pompously, ridiculously, but it's too late, I hear myself saying it: 'I shall be writing about you in my new book.'

He says, 'Who's gonna read it?'

He and his companion turn away to look at the price list in the window of Adam Grooming Atelier, where you can pay a pound a minute for a haircut.

If there's one thing I hate, as a bald man, it's male grooming ateliers.

I walk on to Tate Modern, where they don't have any Yves Klein postcards. So I cross back over the river and walk to Oxfam Bookshop Bloomsbury Street, where I buy a copy of Paul Auster's *The New York Trilogy* previously owned by Gillett. That's all there is, just 'Gillett', no first name or initial. See chapter on *The New York Trilogy*, 'Project For a Walk in New York', for more of this sort of thing.

I shall be writing about you in my new book.

I hear myself saying it over and over. It reminds me of John

Cleese saying to Graham Chapman, 'Tell us about your latest film, Sir Edward.' Cleese, as the interviewer, appealing to the vanity of the famous filmmaker to save the interview after previously jeopardising it by using increasingly over-familiar terms – Edward, Ted, Eddie Baby. Chapman, as the affronted interviewee, drawing the line at Eddie Baby. It's different, obviously, but the connection is the vanity, the pomposity, the self-importance. Mine, I mean.

Talking of interviews, I take my laptop to a café in Stoke Newington to get some work done on this chapter, but a man in a jacket with a VERY LOUD VOICE comes in to talk to a man in a jumper about bookselling.

'On the new book,' says Jumper, 'we must make sure we put enough anecdotes in.'

'Of course,' says Jacket. 'I haven't finished editing. There's some analysis. There's some wisdom and then there's some personal. That's the mix I'm trying to get. There's some really nice stuff there about balance sheets and assets.'

Balance sheets and assets. Where can I pre-order this book?

Jumper is keen to get down to business. 'What are we going to do today?'

'Let's do one more,' says Jacket.

It's one of those French worker's jackets, or baker's jackets, that I like to call Stoke Newington jackets because I see many more of them in N16 than I do in Paris.

Jumper says, 'How about retailers?'

'And how that's changed?' says Jacket enthusiastically. 'Booksellers. Oh and I like your idea that we'll have an epigram.'

I think he says 'epigram'. And I think he means 'epigraph'. But, to be fair, I get them mixed up as well.

'Famous quotes by famous people,' adds Jacket helpfully.

'I absolutely think we should use a Stanley Unwin quote for the whole book,' says Jumper.

I hope he means Professor Stanley Unwin.

'Writing a book is easy,' Jumper paraphrases. 'Printing a book is a harder. Reading a book is harder still. Hardest of all is selling a book.'

Damn. He means publisher Stanley Unwin.

My wife joins me in the café and she's looking so lovely this morning I take a photograph of her, which happens to capture Jumper and Jacket in the background. I send the picture to my friend J, who will probably know who one or both of these gentlemen are. J messages back. The man on the right is R.

R, who previously I was calling Jumper, has started talking about 'TCR' and Jacket asks what TCR is. R isn't sure. He'll call M. M will know. M doesn't answer. R then says he will call S, who does answer.

'Hello, S. I'm here with T. We're working on our new book. Do you know what TCR stands for?'

I can clearly hear S say that M would know and R says he just tried M and he didn't pick up. So, it's still a mystery what TCR stands for, but now I know the names of both these gentlemen, since when R said, 'I'm here with T,' he gave T's full name. I look them up and find they have indeed written a previous book together, and T has published a couple of novels, the first of which I purchase online from Oxfam when I get home, partly because of N's review of the novel, which I find online and which makes it sound like it might be more than worth it.

Just around the corner from the same café, a year earlier, on a road with a path designed for shared use, I was walking and reading Dino Buzzati's short stories. A woman in a green dress on a bike came along and I gestured for her to go first. She said, 'We can go together.' She added, 'Looks like a good book.' I said, 'Dino Buzzati, short stories. Italian, but I'm reading them in French.' She said, 'Well, there you go.' What else could she say? It had been a silly thing for me to have said. Like I was showing off. But I just didn't know what to say. I think I hadn't wanted her to think I was reading them in Italian, in case that had seemed like *really* showing off, as if she might have known that while I'm quite good at French, my Italian is limited to weak chat-up lines last used decades ago. (As I used to joke to two of my oldest friends, Dell and Alison, I knew enough Italian to talk two Italian girls into bed (not at the same time), to which Dell and Alison would respond, 'Two blind Italian girls.')

In spite of feeling foolish regarding the encounter with the woman in the green dress on the bike, I realised I could start collecting – making records of – these interventions from people reacting to my walking and reading.

A couple of weeks later I got slightly lost walking across Tooting Common and reading Patrick Modiano's 2001 novel *La petite bijou*, which I'd bought in its Folio edition from Oxfam Bookshop Chorlton a week earlier, but this meant I encountered Anna from Sweden, on Tooting Bec Road, who stopped me and asked me lots of questions about the book. I told her how much I liked Modiano's books, how they were often about memory, and how relatively simple the French was, in most cases. There was an insistence about her questions, not an impoliteness, but an insistence nevertheless, and she would barely allow me to finish answering one question before asking the next. She was shorter than me, with wavy, dyed blonde hair and carefully applied make-up. She was smartly dressed, with an accent that I couldn't place, but I wouldn't have guessed she was Swedish. I would have said she was from Southeast Asia. She had come to London to visit a friend, she said, as she held on to her shopping trolley. We chatted for five minutes before I made my apologies and twenty yards down the road I came across a second shopping trolley and a number of those large striped bags, like laundry bags, that looked as if they might belong to Anna.

Wednesday 22 November 2023
Brames Books, Halifax.
Middle-aged man in anorak leaving Brames Books with carrier bag, spotting middle-aged woman in facemask, an acquaintance.
Man: I just got some books.
Woman: Not *more* books?
Man: Well, my nephew's doing a psychology degree.
Woman: Ah, proper books.
Man: Yeah, proper books.

I'm walking in south Manchester, from Didsbury to Chorlton, reading *The Voyeur* by Alberto Moravia. The edition is an English translation, an Abacus paperback, with what in the 1990s would have been regarded as an unproblematic cover illustration by Mark Harrison: a naked woman seen from the back. If anyone were to publish an edition of this book today – I'm half way through and can see no reason at all why they might – they might go for a different cover illustration, technically impressive though it is. I'm reading it mostly because I am interested in books that have the same title as other books. Do people talk of such a book sharing a title with another book, in the way that it is often said that I share my name with another writer? (I may even have said it myself.) But, actually, do we share a name or is it more accurate to say that, in this case, there are two writers who have the same name and publish under the same name and I am one of them? If two guests turn up at a dinner party wearing the same red dress, would you say that they are sharing a dress? I don't think so.

I would not say, therefore, that *The Voyeur* by Alberto Moravia and *The Voyeur* by Alain Robbe-Grillet share a title.

I have read the Robbe-Grillet twice. I like his work very much and have read almost all of it, certainly all the fiction. I thought I would like Moravia's novel more than I do. If it weren't for the doubling of the title, I would probably not persevere with it. There's a lot of explicit sex and a lot of rather boring discussion about voyeurism. The poet Kim Moore posted on Twitter that she was looking for representations in male poets' work of female genitalia. I offered her the Mallarmé poem that is quoted in the Moravia and does feel like it's a good fit for the novel. She said it made her feel a little sick.

On the path that runs alongside St Werburgh's Road tram stop, I overtake several members – male and female – of the South Manchester Muslim Walking Group. The name of the group is printed on the backs of the T-shirts some of them are wearing. Once we have all crossed the tram line and are on the path that takes us up to Wilbraham Road, the footsteps behind me grow louder and then quieter, as if someone is trying to catch up with me and then dropping back.

I hear a woman's voice say in a loud whisper to her companion that she 'just [wants] to know what the book is'. I glance back and see a young woman has broken away and is closer to me than the rest of the group. I turn back and keep walking, thinking of the book's title and cover that might not endear it, or me, to the South Manchester Muslim Walking Group and hear another woman's voice saying, 'Ooh, he looked back.' So, I look back again and say hello and the breakaway walker returns the greeting. I explain that I feel slightly compromised by the book's title and cover, showing it to her. She laughs. I explain why I'm reading it, as if the fact that I've chosen to read a second novel called *The Voyeur* is somehow less embarrassing, rather than more embarrassing, than only reading one. She says her son reads and walks and people have told him he shouldn't. She then admits that she used to do the same, but felt it was a bad example to set her children. She says she always has a book in her bag, a book in the car. I ask her about the group. She says the group was formed during lockdown and they kept it going. She tells me her name – Amina – and I tell her mine and later we follow each other on Instagram.

The woman I saw on Wilmslow Road in Withington reading what turned out to be *The Gulag Archipelago* pops up again on Mauldeth Road West. (Cath Staincliffe opens one of her crime novels with the discovery of a body on allotments on Mauldeth Road West and I think I remember her drawing attention to the name, for its containing the words, or the sounds of the words, 'maul' and 'death'. I email Cath to check which novel. She writes back, tells me it's *Blue Murder*, but she doesn't remember discussing the name, 'Mauldeth', and can't find any evidence that she ever did. She suggests I take the credit for it, but I can't. I know I read it, or heard it, somewhere.) The woman is reading again. It's clearly a different book, but I can't see what it is.

I see another woman, in clinical scrubs, on two separate occasions, walking south down Wilmslow Road in West Didsbury, from the direction of the Christie Hospital, at about the same time on each occasion. The first time she's reading *Even Dogs in the Wild* by Ian Rankin and subsequently has moved on to *The Sanatorium* by Sarah Pearse.

I have seen two people walking and reading at Highbury & Islington station in north London: a young man in a red bobble hat, transparent-framed glasses and brown sheepskin coat on the stairs down to the Victoria line reading Hermann Hesse's *Siddharta* (Penguin Modern Classics edition), and a young woman in a black and white check skirt, black top and black and white strappy sandals walking down the steps to the Stratford-bound London Overground platform reading Glennon Doyle's *Untamed: Stop Pleasing, Start Living*.

I've seen two men walking and reading hardback books on Oxford Road in Manchester: a man wearing glasses in his thirties or forties near Oxford Road station reading an unidentified book and a student, possibly an international student, outside the University of Manchester, reading *Colonialism and Development: Britain and Its Tropical Colonies 1850–1960* edited by Michael Havinden and David Meredith. And two women walking and reading hardback books in north London: one in Crouch End, just around the corner from Oxfam Books & Music, in her fifties, wearing a leather jacket, pink scarf, grey skirt and comfortable-looking flat shoes reading Raynor Winn's *The Salt Path* (I tweeted Winn, who was pleased) and one in her twenties or thirties, in black long-sleeved top and leggings, descending a grassy incline on Hampstead Heath completely absorbed in a volume the size of a large dictionary.

Two women survived walking and reading while crossing the road: a woman in a thick grey scarf and green winter coat crossing Whitworth Street West in Manchester not far into a paperback with a largely white cover, and a woman in a red and white check overshirt and blue headscarf reading an Arabic edition of a Harry Potter book and crossing Duncan Terrace in

Islington. To be absolutely honest, she was only about to cross Duncan Terrace when I saw her, having come down Duncan Road from Upper Street, but she looked pretty engrossed, and nothing was coming.

Should I count people reading travel guides? Like the woman on New Oxford Street in London walking and reading a Michelin guide to *Angleterre/Pays de Galles* or the woman on Brick Lane in an 'I ♥ Bad Boys' T-shirt with a Spanish-language guidebook to *Londres*?

Reader-walkers I have seen in Paris have tended to keep their books close to their chests, like the man who looked a bit like James Ellroy in the parc de Belleville or the man who looked a lot more like Jean Yanne in the title role of *Le boucher* in rue de Chabrol – *sans blague* – in the 10th arrondissement, although the woman who closely resembled Gail Ann Dorsey marching confidently down rue de Charonne reading a library copy of the first volume of Leigh Bardugo's *Six of Crows* was an exception.

Sunday 1 February 2009

A way to review a book by Doris Lessing – or to write about her more generally – was to lower yourself into a hot bath that she had previously used. As I climbed in, I noticed an upturned glass bowl on the side, with a blond wig attached to it. This was something she had worn.

In the 1980s and 1990s, when I lived in north London – and later west London – and worked in central London, I would generally take the tube. In the event of a tube strike, I would walk, but that was unusual. When I moved back to Manchester, in the early 2000s, and later started working at Manchester Metropolitan University, trains and trams were inconvenient, and I don't like buses, so I started walking in. When they extended the tram network, I would sometimes get the tram, but the university is a little way out of the city centre, in the direction of home, so it was as if circumstances were conspiring to encourage me to walk.

In lockdown, there was little else to do but walk, mainly around Fog Lane Park, which my wife and I renamed the Exercise Yard. Lockdown, for me, with the constant threat of a potentially serious illness, coincided with a period relatively free from health anxiety or, as my wife calls it, hypochondria. As we emerged from lockdown, however, and were encouraged to perceive the threat from Covid as receding, old anxieties returned. Symptoms queued up like the polite ATM muggers in the Steve Martin vehicle *LA Story*. Instead of 'Hi, my name is Bob. I'll be your robber' I had 'Hi, my name is Skin Lesion. I'll be your possible symptom of skin cancer' or 'Hi, my name is Increased Nocturia. I'll be your possible symptom of prostate cancer' or 'Hi, my name is Changed Bowel Habits. I'll be your possible symptom of bowel cancer'.

These worries teamed up with workplace stress and created a considerable barrier to happiness. One response was to walk in the shadow of this wall, to keep walking, to walk longer and harder, as if I might reach the end of it, but in fact all that happened was I discovered its circularity and walked all the way around it and kept walking, six miles a day, seven, eight, nine, ten miles a day. And then one day the GP uttered the magic words, 'Well, if you're walking ten miles a day, there's no way you've got cancer', and that sealed it. I had to carry on. My ten miles a day were keeping me healthy. Of course, I knew it was more a case of magical thinking than magic words, but I didn't want to test it by falling short.

It wasn't a trudge. I enjoy walking. If I got an order for Nightjars – the short stories I publish in chapbook form via my small press, Nightjar Press – and it was in either Manchester or London, or somewhere I could get to easily in between the two, I no longer relied on Royal Mail, since it had become unreliable, with packages often arriving damaged or incomplete, if they arrived at all, but on Royle Mail. It's cheaper, no orders go missing and there are health benefits. Plus, it caught the imagination of my customers, who still pay P&P charges, aware that they are paying, instead, for my time and lightweight rubber soles.

The difference is you can buy another pair of shoes.

I suppose I wasn't helping matters by so often walking through Southern Cemetery – well, someone stuck it smack in the middle between Didsbury and Chorlton, so I either go around it or right through it, past my dad's grave, listening to the music he loved and wearing his coat and his glasses (glazed with my prescription) and carrying his anxiety around like another precious inheritance. One Sunday evening in July 2023, though, after walking through Hough End Clough in search of the kingfisher I had previously seen as a flash of turquoise above the muddy waters of Red Lion Brook, I marched with a light step along Nell Lane reading boy wonder Victor Jestin's brilliant first novel *Heatwave* (translated by Sam Taylor, but I was reading the original French, *La chaleur*) and turned left on to Burton Road to be hailed by a woman standing outside Saison. She asked me what I was reading and I showed her. It's in French, she said. Yes, I said. Oh, can you read French, she asked. Yes, I said. I studied it at school. Well, I studied it at school, she said. OK, I said, I also studied it at university and continue to read it and speak it whenever possible. What's it about, she asked. It's about a young man on holiday with his family at a campsite, I told her. He witnesses another boy committing suicide. He could perhaps save him, but he doesn't. It's like *L'étranger* for the twenty-first century, I might even have added. He's disaffected, alienated, probably depressed. It's extremely tense. The French is straightforward and the narrative propulsive, making it a quick read.

The woman, who, I was just beginning to realise, had had a couple of drinks, said, Can I tell you about some books? I'd like that, I said, but just one, please, because I have to be home at seven o'clock.

There's a series of books by Kate Mosse, she said. One in particular has to do with travelling back in time. It's a bit weird, she added. But it's quite accurate.

I think she meant 'quite' as in 'very', but it was hard to be certain.

I said it sounded good, but that I had to be home for seven.

She placed her hand on my arm in a way that I could only describe as maternal, despite the fact she was half my age. She probably wouldn't have done it had she not had a couple of drinks, but nevertheless it was a strangely touching gesture. Having recently passed my sixtieth birthday, I had become very aware of my age, so that whenever I sensed that anyone thought I was younger than I was, I felt vaguely encouraged. I'm not saying I look young, but I wonder if being relatively small and slight makes me seem younger than I am. *Seem* rather than *look*. Is there a difference?

It occurs to me also that the people who speak to me when I'm walking and reading, whether or not they've had a couple of drinks, tend to be women. I think I must seem harmless. Maybe women are more outgoing, more generous, more curious? In August 2023, a Sunday again, I was walking to Elizabeth

Gaskell's House reading another French novel, *Anacoluthe* (Calman-Lévy) by Basile Panurgias, which I had bought in the excellent charity bookshop, La vague à l'âme, on rue des Couronnes, in the 20th arrondissement in Paris, the month before.

As I was walking up Ladybarn Lane, approaching Moseley Road, I stepped into the road to overtake a woman in front of me. As I overtook her she asked me what I was reading. I told her it was a novel set in Père Lachaise cemetery in Paris, about a man who writes epitaphs and runs some kind of black market service providing trees for the bereaved to scatter ashes under, if I'd got that right. The language is harder than Victor Jestin's *Heatwave* – difficult vocabulary, lots of slang.

The woman – Lynne-Anne, I would find out later – said she loved looking at old gravestones, so I asked her if she'd been to Père Lachaise. She said she had never been to Paris. She had been to France, but not Paris. She started trying to explain to me where I could see some gravestones further on up the path. I said I thought I knew where she meant. There's a church, or former church, at the end of the path between the Toast Rack and the grammar school. She said if I was walking that way, she would show me, so we walked up Whitworth Lane together. I asked her if she was local. She said she lived on Egerton Road and was going to the Royal Infirmary, where she worked as a nursing assistant, but she was going in to visit her mother who had lymphoma. It won't be long now, Lynne-Anne, her mother had said to her, although she'd already outlived a prediction that she had only two years left, a year ago. Lynne-Anne asked me what I did. I told her. She became excited that I might be famous. I assured her I wasn't. She said she was going to Google me and I explained how there are two writers called Nicholas Royle, so it looks like there are a lot of books by Nicholas

Royle. I wrote the good ones, I told her. I was joking, I added.

Once we'd crossed the bridge over Chorlton Brook, we came to a halt before the former church, which she thought was apartments now, and Lynne-Anne pointed to the gravestones in the former churchyard. She left me and a less friendly-looking nurse came out of the former church and told me that it was a care home and I should return to the path. Could I look at the gravestones, I asked. No, she said, it was private property. I wondered what the law would say if someone with a family connection wanted to visit the gravestones, but I didn't have a family connection and I wanted to get to the book sale at Elizabeth Gaskell's House, which for once I had remembered took place on the second Sunday of the month.

Monday 11 December 2023
Waterstone's, Deansgate, Manchester.
Girl with red hair: Have you read *Animal Farm*?
Girl with brown hair: No.
Girl with red hair: My brother had to read it for a project at school. He came home crying his eyes out. I didn't even know he could read.

On a Friday in September I was walking into town reading Emmanuèle Bernheim's *Stallone* (Folio), which I had bought in the excellent second-hand bookshop Mona Lisait in Paris. Passing through Alexandra Park, I sneezed and a guy sitting on the grass next to another man, who was lying down, looked in my direction. I said, 'Excuse me,' and he said, 'That's all right, man.' I gave him a thumbs-up. Then he said, 'What are you reading?' I said, 'A novel.' He said, 'Come over and tell me about it.' I hesitated a moment, wondering if this was a good idea, then thought, 'It's all good material,' and stepped on to the grass.

I approached the pair and, showing the cover to the young man who had spoken to me, said, 'It's a novel about Sylvester Stallone.'

'That's my name,' he said. 'Sylvester.'

'No way,' I said.

'Swear down, man,' he said. 'Swear down.'

I told him it was about a woman who sees *Rocky III* and it changes her life.

He said, 'Does it include that line?'

'What line?'

'"It's not about how hard you hit. It's about how hard you can get hit and keep moving forward. How much you can take and keep moving forward."'

I said, 'Not yet, but I've not finished it.'

He asked for details so he could look it up. I told him and explained it was in French and possibly not translated. He asked me if I could read French and I said yes and he asked how come. I explained. He asked me to count to five in French. I counted up to five and he repeated it back to me and I said, 'Perfect.'

He then, somewhat surprisingly, complimented me on my outfit. I was wearing a white linen shirt, white trousers, yellow trainers, pink hat, my dad's glasses. I probably looked pretty ridiculous, but I thanked him and told him he was very kind. I said that I had to get on and he said, 'God bless,' and stood up and offered his hand.

I used to think I have a firm handshake. He shook my hand like he was Rocky Balboa and I said it was a pleasure to meet him and continued on my walk, reflecting on the fact that finally a man had talked to me while I was walking and reading.

Then it happened again. A Saturday in October found me

walking north up Essex Road in Islington reading Ian McEwan's *Saturday*. I thought I should at least start it on a Saturday. A man leaned out of a white van driving by and shouted, 'Enjoy your book, sir!' I shouted back, 'Thank you,' though I wasn't sure if I was enjoying it.

I both liked *Saturday* and didn't like it. I think a novel called *Saturday* should be able to be read in its entirety on a Saturday, but it's too long for that. Does the squash game need to go on so long? Does there need to be quite as much musing as there is over the state of the nation/morality of war/arguments for and against invading Iraq? Perowne is a neurosurgeon and therefore, you would think, a clever chap, so why does he think it's a good idea to take the car out, to go a short distance to play squash, on the day of a major demo in central London? He could have saved himself – and the rest of us – a lot of time and aggro. I do, however, like and strongly approve of the obstinate way he consistently refers to the BT Tower as the Post Office Tower.

In November, normal service resumed. I was walking through Withington to MMU to sit on a panel at the National Creative Writing Industry Day and I was reading Peter Farquhar's novel *A Bitter Heart*. A woman cycled up to the Post Office and dismounted. She was chaining up her bike and she said, 'I used to do that.'

I said, 'What? Reading while walking?'

'Yes,' she said. 'I was taking me kids to school and it was like half an hour there and half an hour back, so I was reading, couldn't put it down.'

'Do you not do it any more?' I asked.

'No, I'm on me bike now,' she said.

'Yes,' I said, 'that probably wouldn't be a good idea.'

'There was no smart phones then,' she said, perhaps suggesting that had there been, she would probably have been on her phone.

'Don't spoil it,' I thought.

3

The numbers

The call, from an unrecognised number, comes as I'm having lunch with my wife at home in Manchester.

'Your number's in a book,' says the voice of a young woman.

'What book?' I ask, immediately excited.

'*Man Hating Psycho.*'

Even as I ask who the book is by, I'm aware the title is familiar to me. I will know the answer.

'Virginia.'

That isn't familiar to me. In the background I can hear giggles.

'Where?' I ask, unsure exactly what I'm asking, apart from wanting to keep the conversation going.

'In Waterstone's.'

They probably didn't expect it to last this long and are no doubt already thinking they should hang up. The normal response on the part of whoever answered the call would have been to demand who was calling and to ask, 'How did you get this number?' But they've already told me how they got this number and they happen to have got through to possibly the one person who is delighted to hear that his number is in a book.

'I'm writing about this very thing,' I explain. 'About phone numbers in books. About how if I find a phone number in a book, I mean written in a book, I call it and see who answers.'

I realise they've hung up.

But then a text comes through.

man hating psycho – Iphgenia Baal.

Of course! *Man Hating Psycho* is a short story collection by Iphgenia Baal, one of whose stories I selected for reprint in *Best British Short Stories*. But we communicated by email and never met, and, as far as I can recall, never swopped numbers.

I explain to the caller, now texter, about the book I am writing, and how, with their permission, I'd like to write about this. I learn that there are four of them. They are sixteen and their names are Lucy, Liz, Phoebe and Ammy.

I don't actually own a copy of *Man Hating Psycho*, but I will go out and find one as soon as possible.

Normally, it's the other way around. *I'm* calling or texting a number *I've* found in a book. Not printed in a book, but written in it, usually on the flyleaf, sometimes on the inside front cover or inside back cover, or on the end papers. I wonder what would lead someone to write a number in a book.

Let me give you this book. You'll love it.

Give me your number, so I can let you know what I think of it.

OK. I'll write my number in the book.

Maybe.

In the case of a 1945 hardback copy of Kafka's *The Trial*, a Secker & Warburg edition produced in conformity with war economy standards and stamped on the flyleaf 'Boots College Library', which I bought from Books Peckham in April 2018, the phone number and a name are written on a scrap of paper torn from what looks like an advertising flyer and used as a bookmark (tucked in at page 191). The name is Winston and the number has an 07956 prefix. I compose a text and send it, but it isn't successfully sent.

A Phoenix paperback edition of Iain Sinclair and Dave McKean's *Slow Chocolate Autopsy* that I bought from Oxfam Dalston in March 2012 has a mobile number, prefix 07963, written in ballpoint on the flyleaf. The sevens are crossed. I send a text, which goes green, rather than blue, indicating, as far as I understand it, that the number is assigned to an android phone rather than an iPhone. The attempt to send the text appears to be successful, but no reply comes back. Or at least not yet.

Tuesday 4 October 2022
Oxfam, Kenilworth, Warwickshire.
Volunteer: How are you getting on with your hearing aids?
Customer: [. . .]

Monday 10 July 2023. Paris. I wake up in a hotel in the 20th arrondissement, which is fine, because that was where I went to sleep the night before. A few months earlier I read a short novel by Cees Nooteboom, *The Following Story*, given to me for my birthday by Gareth Evans, in which the narrator wakes up in a hotel room in Lisbon having gone to bed in Amsterdam, so I understand that waking up where I went to sleep can no longer be taken for granted. It is the last day of a long weekend in Paris. After a relaxed breakfast I check out of the hotel, leaving my bag, and walk to the 3rd arrondissement. Over the weekend I have been exploring Paris's celebrated covered passages for a story I want to write for a new collection, *Paris Fantastique*. I was surprised by how quiet the covered passages were and thought I should see if they're any busier on a weekday, although

I know that Monday in Paris scarcely counts as a weekday. I also want to go to the 8th. I read an interview in the *Guardian* with Roman Polanski in which the journalist, Sue Summers, revealed – unless it had been revealed before (can you reveal something that has already been revealed?) – where the director lives. I am very nosy about where people live – or lived. When I obtained the address of writer and film-maker Alain Robbe-Grillet, in Neuilly-sur-Seine, I went there, on an earlier visit to Paris, on a sort of pilgrimage. I went to look at the grave of Sartre and De Beauvoir in the Cimetière de Montparnasse and found that I am more excited by going to see where people live – or lived – rather than where they lie at rest.

Polanski's apartment building is on avenue Montaigne, above a bank. It's cool and modern. I imagine him having a whole floor, though I don't know which one. I picture him popping out for a pint of milk, or a pair of Jimmy Choos, since the footwear firm is next door, as well as, confusingly, over the road, presumably to catch those customers too rich to be arsed to cross the road.

Polanski doesn't pop out.

Next stop is 39 rue de Calais in the 9th, the address on a letter addressed to Simone Choule in *The Tenant*, Polanski's 1976 film of Roland Topor's novel first published in 1964. On the way to rue de Calais I stop briefly at a street bookseller on place de Clichy and buy, for one euro, a 2008 Folio edition of Sylvie Germain's novel *Le livre des nuits*. I met Germain once, many years ago, possibly introduced by Pete Ayrton at a Serpent's Tail event, but the main reason why I buy her book is for an inclusion I find in it, at page 20, a small-format black-and-white photograph of an artist at work in his studio. He appears to have both hands on a large canvas on the wall and, oddly, both feet off the floor. The book also has a name and number on the flyleaf, in pencil.

The name is Donnard; the number, that of a French mobile, has an 0683 prefix.

Back home a few days later, I text the number, in French. After three hours, I receive a reply, also in French. Emmanuelle Donnard writes: 'If this story is true, it's very amusing. Sometimes, it seems, a message in a bottle arrives in port.' The translation is mine and I'm uncertain about it because 'une bouteille à la mer' can mean either a message in a bottle or a cry for help and is she referring to her number in the book or to my message to her? She goes on to say she hasn't read the book and doesn't know who it might have belonged to. She asks to see the photo of the artist in the studio. I send her a picture of it. It doesn't ring any bells, but she did study art, and leaving her contact details in a book was the kind of thing she would do. I send her a picture of the flyleaf – her name and number. She confirms that she remembers neither the book, nor the person to whom it might have belonged. She adds that she has led a life full of encounters and that my story has captured her imagination. We switch our correspondence to email. The handwriting is not hers, she says. The book most likely belonged to a former lover.

Emmanuelle, now 43, lived in Paris between 2004 and 2017 in the 18th near Jules Joffrin. She would go out around place de Clichy and Pigalle. Having studied education and political science, she became a designer and is now a researcher in innovation in pedagogy at the University of Paris. The identities of both the former owner of the book and the artist in the photograph remain unknown.

When I finally make it to rue de Calais, in search of No. 39, it doesn't exist. The street only goes up to No. 25.

Tuesday 4 October 2022

Tree House Bookshop, Kenilworth, Warwickshire.

First male customer: Don't read that book if you're feeling a bit down.

Second male customer: What, *The Road*? Bleak, isn't it?

First male customer: Yeah.

[First male customer leaves shop.]

Second male customer: I like American novelists. Like Tom Wolfe. *The Right Stuff*. About the astronauts. Kind of gives you an idea of what it was like.

Bookseller: Absolutely.

Not all of my adventures arising from phone numbers in books are as rewarding as that involving Emmanuelle.

On Wednesday 15 February 2023, I walked from Stoke Newington to Kentish Town reading Patrick Modiano's 1990 novel *Honeymoon*. (I was reading a French edition, original title *Voyage de noces*, in Folio paperback, with a handwritten reminder in the back about a poetry reading by Dinah Livingstone at Conway Hall in Red Lion Square on Saturday 27 October – it could have been 2012 or 2018. There's also an email address and a phone number for the Humanist Library, run by the Ethical Society, at Conway Hall. In the novel, Jean goes missing from his own life in Paris in order to unravel the story behind the suicide of a Frenchwoman in Milan. He's confident his wife will not miss him, as she is cheating on her lover, one of Jean's colleagues, with another of his colleagues. It's classic Modiano: loss, memory, melancholy; evocative descriptions of rooms and streets and the fall of light. There's also a moment in which another character, Rigaud, tears the flyleaf out of a Série Noire crime novel and writes his name on it to give to Jean.) In Kentish Town, in

Oxfam Books & Music, I find a Folio edition of another French novel, Marguerite Duras's *The Little Horses of Tarquinia*, with a name and phone number, Vincent in Marseille, written on the inside back cover. I try texting – no response – and calling, but get an automated message: 'The number you have called is not recognised. Please check the number. If you need help, call the operator on 100 from your mobile.'

In October 2023, in Oxfam Books & Music Crouch End, I found a copy of Steve Erickson's brilliant 2007 novel *Zeroville* with a name and number on the flyleaf. The prefix was 01453, the name Eco. I imagined an Italian intellectual holed up in the English countryside trying to write a book and seeking distraction by reading *Zeroville*. I Googled the number just to make sure it wasn't something boring.

It was something boring, but at least they're boring and green. Ecotricity – apparently 'Britain's greenest energy supplier'. I didn't call them, but I might do if Scottish Power's rates continue to rise at the current rate.

In the same month, back in Oxfam Books & Music Kentish Town, where something of interest always seems to turn up, I found a Virago Modern Classics edition of *The Judge* by Rebecca West containing, at page 139, a set of largely illegible (book group?) notes, with an address on King Henry's Road and a phone number – 0761 232970 – that doesn't work. Who knows if it ever did? It seems to be missing a digit.

Another sage-green Virago Modern Classics edition from another Oxfam Books & Music: Stevie Smith's *Novel on Yellow Paper*, found in the Kentish Town shop in February 2019, contains, at page 49, a page from a memo pad from the Golden Age of Athens, a boutique hotel in the Greek capital, with a UK landline number written on it in ballpoint, incorporating the international prefix. I call the number – a London number – in October 2023 and the call is answered by a gentleman working for Haggie Partners, which appears to be one of those firms – a 'leading communications consultancy in the global financial services sector' – whose function and activities I will never fully, or even partly, understand. 'Used skilfully,' their website continues, 'communication is a dynamic business tool that will raise brand awareness and market profile, attract and retain business and talent, bolster reputations, inform stakeholders and shape opinions.' A short conversation establishes that neither of us can cast any light on why Haggie Partners' number was written on that piece of hotel stationery slipped inside *Novel on Yellow Paper*.

More international connections arise from within the pages of a Picador edition of Colm Tóibín's *The Story of the Night* purchased from Oxfam Bookshop Muswell Hill in June 2017. At page 137 there's a business card for the Riding House Café in Fitzrovia. On the reverse of the business card are two US landline numbers, one in pencil, one in ballpoint, both with Miami prefixes. Indeed, the word 'Miami' has been added, in pencil, under the first number. When I call that number I get a 'Call failed' notification. With the second number I find that I'm able to send a WhatsApp message – apparently you can send a WhatsApp to a landline (who knew?) – which appears to be received by a young woman with long wavy dark-brown hair. She doesn't respond and so I leave it.

I find another business card with a handwritten phone number on it inside another Steve Erickson novel, *Arc d'X*. It's the Vintage paperback edition of this extraordinary novel that I read when it came out in hardback in 1994 and can't remember a thing about apart from how good it was. I had been following Erickson's career since buying his first novel, *Days Between*

Stations, in a gorgeous paperback edition – either the US Vintage Contemporaries edition or the UK edition from Futura, both featuring Rick Lovell's surreal illustration of a black panther in a desert landscape awash with moonlight. The business card, at page 65 in *Arc d'X*, has on it a photograph of a woman wearing a tight corset. On her right leg is printed JAY • HAIR • MAKE • UP. There's a number, crossed out, and written alongside, in fine black felt tip, is an 071 landline number. When I call the equivalent of that number, hoping to find out if Jay still does hair and make-up, it rings and rings. I leave it ringing for a while, then hang up. (Eighteen pages further on in the same copy of *Arc d'X* I find a piece of paper with, in blue ballpoint, a quote from Christopher Marlowe's *The Jew of Malta*: 'I count religion but a childish toy, and hold there is no sin but ignorance.')

On Friday 21 April 2023 I travelled by train to Kenton, then walked to Harrow to deliver Nightjars to Michael Middleton, who aspires to direct Disney films and in the meantime is a 'keen director and editor of corporate media and music videos as well as [his] own drama short films in [his] own time', according to his LinkedIn page, from which I quote with his permission. Harrow was weird – in a good way or a bad way, depending on your point of view – totally dominated by its famous school, in the way that the village where K arrives in Kafka's *The Castle* is dominated by, indeed indivisible from, the castle. I walk past businesses that appear moribund; you imagine them trying to take off, or take root, but finding it impossible for some reason in the shadow of the school. On the school's endless playing fields I see green woodpeckers and I remember that the only other time I've seen green woodpeckers in this country was on the campus lawns at the University of Kent. Green woodpeckers spend most of their time on the ground, because they have an appetite for ants, as well as, it would seem, a thirst for knowledge.

I walked back to Kenton and got the tube to Charing Cross. From there I walked to various south London addresses delivering Nightjars, rewarding myself with a visit to Oxfam Bookshop Herne Hill, where I bought, among other items that may crop up in other chapters, the biggest, heaviest and, on the face of it, least-interesting-to-me book I've ever bought from a charity shop, but I simply couldn't resist *Standard Arabic* (Cambridge), by Eckehard Schulz, Günther Krahl and Wolfgang Reuschel. The reason? The astonishing inclusions at page 527.

A Google Maps map of Cairo with one location pinpointed with a green arrow; a circular to tutors/trainers attending a meeting, with a handwritten phone number for a 'Guardroom' (with a Portsmouth prefix); a 'DS Timeline for Walk-In Exercise' (for five role-players); half a page including further notes (items 11 and 12 – so 1–10 are missing); a handwritten diagram/flow chart that mentions certain places, time-frames and names, including the *nom de guerre* of one of Osama Bin Laden's twelve bodyguards. I called the Guardroom number and it was answered by a man's voice saying, simply, 'Hello?' I asked if I had reached the Guardroom and he confirmed that I had before asking me who I was and why I was calling. If I had hoped to get much material out of him, I would have been disappointed. The conversation was short and to the point.

Still, that's more fun than 'The number you have called is not recognised . . .', which is what I get when I call the number for 'Paul' I found written on a twice-folded piece of memo paper from the Department For Trade and Industry at page 13 of Will Hutton's *The State We're In* (Vintage) that I bought from Oxfam Blackheath on Sunday 7 January 2018 and when I tried dialling the number for 'Kathy at work' written on the back of a London Transport bus ticket dated 23 January 1997 that I found at page 37 of a Picador edition of Tama Janowitz's *Slaves of New York* that I bought from Oxfam Books & Music Islington on Monday 12 April, 2021, the day that non-essential shops were allowed to open after the third national coronavirus lockdown.

There's no shortage of second-hand bookshops where you can sit and enjoy your purchases over a hot drink – one thinks of Scarthin Books, Astley Book Farm, Greenhouse Books, Didsbury Bookshop, Westwood Books, Bookcase, Burley Fisher and many more – but I can only think of two where one is routinely offered to you, on the house, the moment you enter. One – Goldmark Books in Uppingham – is no more (swallowed up by Goldmark Gallery). The other is Archive Bookstore, on Bell Street in Marylebone, central London. To be accurate, I have only been there twice in thirty years and it was only on my most recent visit – Monday 30 October 2023 – that I was offered tea on arrival, but it was offered in such a way that it seemed to me likely that it was offered to everyone all day long. I can't vouch for this. If you go and you are not offered tea, please don't blame me, or owner Tim Meaker. Well, if you must blame anyone, blame me. Tim Meaker should remain entirely blameless. And what tea it was! A blend, he said, of two teas, but I can't remember what either of them was. Fresh milk was offered and accepted – and biscuits, from a tin donated by a customer.

I heard myself apologising for not having visited the shop for about thirty years, completely forgetting that I had last been there in September 2017, when I had found a Picador to add to my collection, Roy Heath's *The Murderer* (complete with inclusion, the author's obituary from the *Guardian*, written by

Margaret Busby, publisher and now president of English PEN), and had even made a note about the 'nice man running the shop' and how pleased he had been that other customers and I had been buying books. It is a not-uncommon experience that I hear myself going on and on and fervently wish that I could edit my speech in real time, that I could select a chunk of it and replace it with a couple of better-chosen words.

Luckily, another customer arrived to shut me up. Dave, from South Wales, a fire breather for eighteen years, was looking for books on magic tricks. While he enjoyed a cup of tea, I went and had a look at the relatively small paperback section. Archive Bookstore is one of those second-hand bookshops that my wife will not enter – or she will turn around and leave the moment she has entered. They appear to be held up, just about, by books. There are enormous piles, almost drifts, of books. Books on shelves, books on chairs or stools, books on the counter, or books in place of a counter. She didn't last long in Morecambe's Old Pier Bookshop. I daren't take her in Halewood & Son in Preston. She would like Tim Meaker, but she would not like his bookshop, whereas I love it.

While I was checking the paperbacks for shadow lines, I heard something that took me back thirty years, to when I visited Christopher Kenworthy in his shared house in Bath to work on edits to my first novel, *Counterparts*, which he had foolishly agreed to publish on his Barrington Books list. As we worked on the text, I was vaguely aware of someone in another part of the house idly picking out random notes on an old piano. When I later wrote to Chris and recalled this, he explained that the music – Michael Nyman's *1–100*, as played by Piano Circus – had been coming from a cassette player under his bed.

Did Tim Meaker have the Nyman piece, which I'm listening

to as I write these words, playing through hidden speakers? No, there's a piano in the cellar and customers are welcome to go downstairs and make use of it.

I bought two books – Laurence Sterne's *A Sentimental Journey* (Everyman) for its inclusion, at page 41, a scrap of paper with a name, A & D West, and a phone number, 0171 387 9300, and *Hotel Savoy* (Picador Classics) by Joseph Roth. When I Google, later, what I understand to be the modern-day equivalent of 0171 387 9300 – 020 7387 9300 – I see that it appears to be the main switchboard number for University College Hospital, but when I call it to check, I get the recorded message, 'It has not been possible to connect your call. Please try again later.'

Popping out – or bobbing out as we say around our way – for last-minute shopping before the Christmas madness, I found myself torn between two Tescos. Burnage or East Didsbury? I know what you're thinking. Neither. Go to Aldi. Or M&S. Anywhere rather than Tesco. But there was something I needed I knew I wouldn't find anywhere local other than Tesco, so Tesco it was, but which one? I opted for Burnage, as they have a charity book table. I'm not sure what charity they're supporting – it doesn't say on the collecting box – but surely you can trust Tesco? Dame Shirley Porter? Westminster cemeteries scandal? Homes for votes scandal? So 1980s. The thing is, my ex-wife once left her purse in a trolley at Burnage and someone handed it in, so I have a soft spot for Burnage.

Books with phone numbers written in are like buses, apparently. It had been a few weeks since I'd found one and now three came along at once. It was like they'd seen me coming. Here he comes, he'll be unable to resist us and he's got no change, so he'll have to stick a fiver in the money box and then he'll worry that a bit of it is sticking out, because it's quite full and needs emptying, and he'll worry that someone might be tempted to remove it, and so he might attempt that himself, in order to go and get change instead, and then he'll worry that he's being caught on CCTV appearing to try to steal the contents of the charity money box and so he'll quickly let go.

The first one to catch my eye, since I'd never read this writer and had always been curious, was Tom Sharpe's *Porterhouse Blue* (Pan), with an 07703 number written on the inside back cover. Secondly, *The Secret Crown* (Penguin) by Chris Kuzneski with an 07908 number, preceded by the partial word 'Elec', written on the flyleaf. And lastly, *Hopeless Romantic* (Bold Strokes Books) by Georgia Beers, a writer of lesbian romance, whose name, I must admit, I had not come across before. The number, with an 07460 prefix, was on the flyleaf again. I couldn't find the latter on WhatsApp, so I texted the number. It went as an iMessage and was 'delivered', but not 'read'. When I put the *Porterhouse Blue* number into WhatsApp it came up with a name and a profile picture. My message got two ticks and the profile pic promptly disappeared. I'm not the world's smartest WhatsApp user, but it didn't take a genius to work out that she had blocked me, which was fair enough, I suppose.

Porterhouse Blue had a big corner turned down on page 39. I started reading the novel walking back from Burnage and didn't get that far. I gave up after seven pages, at the end of chapter one.

I WhatsApped 'Elec', whose number was in the front of the fantasy novel by Chris Kuzneski, and Andy Jackson of AWJ Electrical – fully qualified Stroma-certified electrician with more then ten years' experience in the domestic sector – was kind enough to reply. We decided someone must have given Andy's number to the owner of the book and he or she had reached for the first thing to hand on which to write the number.

I know who I'll be contacting next time I need an electrician.

In the meantime, I get my hands on a copy of Iphgenia Baal's *Man Hating Psycho* (Influx Press) in Blackwells and it doesn't take me long to find the story featuring my number – and a lot of other numbers. The story is called 'Change:)' and takes the form of a transcription of an online chat in which a character called Red Ed creates a group to discuss politics. Following his opening address, numerous individuals, identified only by their phone numbers, leave the group. A handful of others chip in, me, with a name I don't recognise and a phone number I do, among them. My contribution is so boringly sensible and pragmatic I can almost imagine myself saying it in real life.

In fact, I start to wonder if perhaps I did say it in real life.

I email the author and she confirms that I did, in a group chat created by a mutual acquaintance to which I finally remember contributing. 'The numbers and chat are (mostly) real,' Iphgenia tells me, adding that she made up the names to disguise the identities of real people.

I'm reminded of a line from Iphgenia Baal's list story '99 Customer Journey Horror', in which every line – indeed, every item in the list – ends with the word 'horror'. It appeared in *Denizen of the Dead: The Horrors of Clarendon Court* (Cripplegate Books) edited by Stewart Home and was reprinted in *Best British Short Stories 2021*. '4. Being part of something special horror.' (It makes sense in context.) Had it not been for Iphgenia Baal's singular imagination and inclination to try out experimental narrative techniques, I may never have had the privilege of encountering Lucy, Liz, Phoebe and Ammy.

4

Unread books

Writer and retired teacher of creative writing Robert Graham said to me, when my wife and I found ourselves sitting next to him at a Sparks concert in Manchester's Bridgewater Hall, that what he liked about *White Spines* was the kindness I showed in it.

Robert Graham, look away now.

I found a second-hand proof copy of a novel by someone who in my opinion is a rather average writer. Their ideas are uninteresting and their execution of them is unexceptional – their prose is mediocre – but they have come to enjoy a certain level of success. (I am using 'they' not because it is a preferred pronoun, but for discretion.) This would be bearable were it not for this writer's somewhat irritating public persona, which does not exclude humble bragging and faux humility. The proof copy of the novel was only 50p, because it was heavily annotated, most likely by a reviewer in preparation for writing a review. I would have happily paid £5 for it. I haven't read the novel but I have read the annotations in the proof, which I suspect are far more interesting and much funnier. Even if you are not writing comic fiction, your novel should surely still be funny, now and again, just like life is, even if it's only bitterly funny. The annotations in this proof have got me through several long, dark nights. I don't doubt that there are proof copies of my own novels out there, or finished copies, similarly annotated, similarly taken apart and crushed to tiny fragments, and there may be people who would take pleasure in finding them and I wouldn't begrudge them that pleasure for a moment. But, for now, the pleasure is all mine. And, I hope, yours.

To kick off, the Reviewer underlines half a paragraph a few pages in and adds a note: 'This is much more like the sort of writing [the Author] previously seemed to deride . . .' This is followed by a few pages of underlinings, question marks, circled phrases, whole paragraphs placed between giant parentheses that seem to suggest redundancy. A character speaks 'like nobody speaks'; 'none of this is plausible'; 'kitsch'. 'A propos of fuck all,' writes the Reviewer about a particular passage of dialogue. Repetitions, contradictions and oxymorons are circled and underlined. 'Descriptive powers on the blink,' the Reviewer writes. You can almost see the Reviewer's eyes rolling and is that a sigh causing the Reviewer's shoulders to rise and fall?

Voice is 'all over the place' and subject to 'bizarre swerves'. The novel is 'underpowered' and 'lacks much sense of internal propulsion'. Short words are proposed in the margin, to take the place of combinations of longer words in the text.

About 100 pages in, the Reviewer is becoming exasperated. Alongside an exchange of dialogue, we read, 'FFS.'

FFS was the name given to the supergroup formed when Franz Ferdinand and Sparks decided to collaborate on an album, also called *FFS*, but it seems unlikely the Reviewer is referring to either.

As we move, with some relief, into the final third, the

Reviewer finds that the novel 'lacks the energy of [the Author's] previous work'. Alongside a reference to time moving very slowly the Reviewer adds, 'I know how [the Character] feels,' and half a page later a couple of lines are underlined and a single word added in the margin: 'Jesus.'

A few pages later, patience with the plot is running out: 'This is ludicrous.' Indeed, the Reviewer has had enough: the last thirty-odd pages are mostly free of notes.

I have left out a lot of more specific remarks so that the novel under review – and its author – should remain unidentifiable, because it's not about bashing an individual. Don't we all know someone who, in our opinion, is not as good as (annoyingly large numbers of) people seem to think they are? Maybe they've won prizes or critical acclaim or achieved huge sales or had their work adapted for film or TV, or all of these things, and don't we sometimes think, even if they live at the other end of the country, This town ain't big enough for both of us?

Saturday 30 July 2022
St Vincent de Paul Society, Kingsland Road, Dalston, London. Couple in their sixties, shorts, sunglasses around neck.
Him [pulling out Marlon James's *A Brief History of Seven Killings*]: I started this book. I don't know where it is but I don't have it any more.
Her: And now you can finish it.
Him: Yes.

Ever since she read my sort-of campus novel, *First Novel* (Vintage), my wife has been urging me to read Malcolm Bradbury's *The History Man*. I find a copy in the basement of Housmans, a not-for-profit bookshop at the King's Cross end of Caledonian Road in central London. As a not-for-profit writer, also running an effectively not-for-profit small press, I feel at home in a not-for-profit bookshop. The reality, probably, is that most bookshops are not-for-profit, even those that strive not to be. On the ground floor, Housmans sells new books, of a radical nature, while in the basement you'll find a smallish second-hand section. That's where, in December 2022, I find a copy of *The History Man*. To be honest, I've seen and not bought other copies of Bradbury's 1975 campus novel that was made into a TV series in 1981, but this is the first one I've seen with a clear shadow line along the top edge of the book block.

The inclusion is a love letter, from R to R. (I'm sorry, but both first names begin with 'R'.) It starts with a quote attributed to Chet Baker, but which is actually from a song written by Cassandra Wilson, 'You Don't Know What Love Is'. The content of the letter is forward looking, optimistic. I hope things worked out, in spite of the title of the Cassandra Wilson composition.

They don't work out for me with *The History Man*. I fail to finish very few books these days, partly because I'm very careful to avoid starting books I think I might not finish. I mention to a few people, including my wife, the trouble I'm having with it: I find it rather tedious. I don't like the style; the content feels very old fashioned. One distinguished author sticks up for it on Twitter. DJ Taylor says it's 'a classic exposé of some of the limits of liberalism'. Everybody else says I should watch the TV adaptation. Maybe I will. But I won't be finishing the novel, which will remain, for me, an unread book.

Other unread books include any publications by authors whom I asked – nicely, politely, occasionally via mutual contacts – for jacket quotes for novels, when I was acquiring books, often debut novels, for Salt Publishing during the 2010s, who couldn't even be bothered to write back and decline. Especially if the writer had asked me to approach them specifically because they were a big fan, a detail I would always pass on, or they are, according to their Wikipedia page, a 'practising Christian'. Yes, I'm looking at you, ██ ██, and at you, ██████ ██████.

Saturday 21 January 2023
Oxfam Shop Dalston, Kingsland Road, Dalston, London.
Young couple looking for book as present.
Her [pulling out hardback of Richard Osman's *The Thursday Murder Club*]: How about this? This is, like . . .
Him: Is it, like . . . Have you heard of it?
Her [putting it back]: Yes,
Him: I think it's, like, too childish?
[She pulls out *Unexploded* by Alison MacLeod. He has a look at it. They leave books and go and look at clothes.]

First Novel, actually my seventh, was going to be followed by *Second Album* (and, later, *Third Act*), but I made a schoolboy error by sharing an early draft of the opening chapter of *Second Album* with a group of creative writing MA students. We had a free week and they asked and I thought what harm can it do? It might be helpful.

It wasn't.

One of the students – let's call him D – made what I thought were some harsh criticisms and a short while later I abandoned the novel. A bit rich, you might think, the tutor finding himself unable to follow the advice he would give to his students, to sift criticism for nuggets, leaving aside the dirt and grit. Maybe I had my own doubts about it? Anyway, I dropped the project and haven't written a novel in ten years, the longest gap since I started writing forty years ago. The upside is I wrote more short stories than I might otherwise have done and I love the short story more than I love the novel, as both reader and writer, so that's good, but it's hard to build a career on short stories, unless you're as concise and effective as Lydia Davis or can get away with condensing novels into forty pages and calling them short stories like Alice Munro.

Fast forward to 2022. Through the window of a charity bookshop I visit occasionally, I see D. He's behind the counter. I can't face the conversation. Q: *Are you still writing that novel?* A: *No, I abandoned it after those remarks you made.* Either one of those lines could be assigned to either one of us, since his picking holes in my work had been preceded by my finding fault with his, as part of my job.

I walk on.

Fast forward again to April 2023. I'm peering through the window of the same charity shop. D has been making my life more interesting by popping up in two branches of this particular charity shop chain, both branches that I would occasionally visit. The coast appears to be clear, so I enter and immediately become aware of D, who had somehow been obscured by one of the displays. He hasn't seen me, but the volunteer behind the till has, so I can hardly turn around and leave. It's a bright, cold spring day, so I am wearing a woolly hat and scarf and coat. The photochromic lenses of my glasses, which were dark when I entered the shop, are already becoming less dark as I approach the bookshelves and will become lighter the longer I stay. D is bound to recognise me. Especially if I buy anything, like the copy of Salman Rushdie's *Shame* with the Brooke Bond Tea card used as a bookmark. As a child, I collected Brooke Bond

Tea cards, you won't be surprised to learn, and this one is from a set I am not familiar with. The former owner of the book has written her name on the inside front cover – Deborah Ann Turton. The albedo of the white card of the inside front cover, Deborah Ann Turton's name notwithstanding, is approaching 0.9, that of fresh snow, as the molecules on my lenses complete the alteration of their structure back to transparency and I put the book back on the shelf and, head down, pretend to take a phone call and flee the shop.

Fast forward to September 2023. Once again I find myself peering through the window of the charity shop in question. Only when I am satisfied that D is definitely not on the shop floor – there's a young man behind the till and bending down I can see no ankles poking down below the free-standing bottom shelves – do I enter. I pass the doorway that leads to the stairs up to the first floor – staff only – and immediately start spotting books with shadow lines. As I pick out F Scott Fitzgerald's *Bernice Bobs Her Hair* (Penguin Modern Classics) with an inclusion at page 107, a business card for sales director Andy Hawthorne of Nick Stone Accessories Ltd, which joins the duplicate Picador edition of Russell Hoban's *Pilgermann* signed by the author to 'Pog' that I have already selected, I hear footsteps coming downstairs. D appears in the doorway and crosses the floor to join the volunteer at the till.

How badly do I want an F Scott Fitzgerald with Andy Hawthorne's business card? Can I survive without the signed Russell Hoban?

It sounds like the volunteer is new. D is giving him advice on shop-keeping. In a minute, surely, D will return to whatever he was doing upstairs, leaving the volunteer to deal with customers on his own. To deal with *this* customer, who senses that D has spotted him and is waiting to see what he – the customer – will do. He – D – probably saw me on the CCTV while he was upstairs and came down deliberately. Walking out without buying anything no longer feels like an option.

One of the pair crosses the floor of the shop and goes upstairs. It's not D, who remains behind the counter. I pretend to continue looking at the shelves, but all I can see is future-me walking to the till and placing the two books I want to buy on the counter. I know it's going to happen. It happens. D looks at me with an amused smile. It's his default smile, I tell myself. He doesn't recognise me.

'All right?' he asks. It's the kind of question he would ask any customer.

'Yes, thanks,' I say. 'How are you?' Maybe I would say that to any bookseller?

He tells me the total. I tap my card. We say goodbye and I leave the shop.

Monday 23 March 2009
Someone, not me, is rewriting an existing series of crime novels. The main differences are that the first book in the series will appear in a small format and the protagonist, presumably some kind of detective figure, will be black, whereas formerly he was white. The author doing the rewrites is a woman. I am eager to get a look at the results.

In August 2023, my wife and I were in France, staying with friends. One day, my old friend Brian drove us to Périgueux in the Dordogne where we visited the market and I had a quick look at the second-hand bookshop where last time I was there I found Marie Redonnet's *Forever Valley* (Editions de Minuit) and became an instant fan. This time I found another Minuit book, one of their smaller Double editions, *Loin d'eux* by Laurent Mauvignier. Next we went to Bordeilles and had a picnic by the river. We saw three kingfishers, or one kingfisher three times. On to Brantôme, where we found Bookstop, a lovely second-hand bookshop and café and gallery – a great combination – run by an Englishman called Howard.

In the garden at Bookstop, we encountered Chris Pearson, an artist, taking down his show of paintings and sculptures, one of which was a wicker man called *Atomic Frank* reading a copy of *The Frank Muir Book* (Heinemann). We chatted to Chris and I emailed him later. He said he had asked Howard for his worst book and Howard had given him a book about motor racing, but when they opened it they found it was signed, so Howard took it back and gave Chris *The Frank Muir Book* instead, which was much more apt because the sculpture was mounted on a wall – *mur* in French.

In the bookshop Howard had a copy of my award-winning novel *The Matter of the Heart*. (So what if it was the Bad Sex in Fiction Award?) I bought two books by Buzzati – *Le K* (Livre de Poche) and *Nous sommes au regret de* . . . (Points), which contained an inclusion, a boarding pass in the name of Olivier des Clers – and Christian Oster's *Trois hommes seuls* (Minuit).

Chris told me about a work in progress. 'I have been working for some time on a sculpture made entirely of books that I have shrouded in resin to protect them from the weather. The idea was for it to be mounting the ledge above the river at the Bookstop, a shelf of books with the books at one end tumbling forward and many more books tumbling and turning but just before they reach the water they open up and fan out into swooping birds

. . . I have been having a few logistical problems with the resin process, but will get there.'

I look forward to going back and seeing that when it is finished.

More unread books.

Any book I haven't already read by any author who, when invited to read for five minutes at an event, asks if they can read for seven minutes and then reads for thirty-five minutes.

Any book by an author who, when asked by an impoverished fan to sign an old paperback at a launch for their unaffordable new hardback, refuses.

Any book by an author popular with readers but unpopular with publicists and editors. (There's usually a good reason for that unpopularity.)

Any reprint anthology put together by an editor who refuses to print credits acknowledging where a story was first published, rather than where they happened to see it reprinted.

Any book from a particular small independent press whose publisher refuses to supply another small independent press with a digital file of an out-of-print collection by a deceased author whose work is being reissued by that second small independent press.

Any book by an author who, when an editor emails them asking if he may reprint a short story in *Best British Short Stories*, doesn't respond. Even when he emails them on two different email addresses as well as via their agent, who doesn't respond either. (It's hard to understand why an author would not want their story to be reprinted in a collection called *Best British Short Stories* – even if they wish the publisher were bigger or the editor more prestigious – and if they are not sufficiently imaginative to come up with a good reason for their story's inclusion, perhaps they could think of the boost it would give to lesser-known writers to be featured alongside a writer of their stature.)

Don't cut off your nose to spite your face, I seem to hear the odd voice say. *Don't be prejudiced. Don't be this. Don't be that.*

If we can agree that it's impossible to read everything, then we have to choose which books to read and which books to leave on the shelf. Assuming the act of choosing is more sophisticated than flipping a coin, it is surely not unreasonable to apply criteria. For mine, see above. I'll read just about any other adult fiction. Apart from historical fiction, romance, and novels over 400 pages long (with exceptions).

On a Friday at the end of September 2023 I visited a second-hand bookshop in the north of England. That's unusually vague, you may be thinking. Yes, it is, deliberately so, because what follows is kind of a bad review and there's not a great deal of point in being specific. Things might improve – you never know. I hope so.

I started the day in Sedbergh, which, if it weren't for Westwood Books and Clutterbooks, would be a little disappointing as England's book town, lagging some way behind those of Scotland and Wales. In Clutterbooks I bought Marilyn Robinson's *Housekeeping*, a great novel, but not a nice edition.

My favourite edition of *Housekeeping* is the 1982 King Penguin edition – 187 pages – with a lovely cover illustration by Emma Chichester-Clark, two girls sitting by a window, curtains blowing in the breeze. The 2009 Virago edition I buy in Westwood Books – 339 pages, with sepia photographic cover, an empty rocking chair by a window (more wind-blown curtains) – somehow contrives to end up more than twice as thick as the

King Penguin despite the type definitely looking smaller and less inviting to read.

I bought it for its inclusion, a Hallmark card (a dog sitting by a door that's ajar) from S to J, at page 199, in which S wrote, 'Dear [J], I love you so very, very much. You are my life, [S] xxx.'

Incidentally, a month earlier, in Burley Fisher in Hackney, I had found a Penguin Classics edition of Emile Zola's novel *Nana* with an inclusion, at page 327: a receipt for an order of travellers cheques in the name of Emma Chichester-Clark.

Back in Westwood Books, I bought two more books I had no interest in for their inclusions: Nora Roberts' *Stars of Fortune* (Piatkus) and Ruth Prawer Jhabvala's *In Search of Love and Beauty* (Penguin). The former had a poignant letter, also at page 327, from Alice to her Grandma and Da and a booking slip for a hospital meal for a Jean; *In Search of Love and Beauty* contained a business card, at page 185, in the name of Jean Carroll, Principal, Dunfermline College of Phys Ed, Edinburgh.

Leaving Sedbergh, I drove over (through? Across?) the Forest of Bowland (surprisingly few trees) and parked on the outskirts of a Lancashire town and walked back in to visit a second-hand bookshop. I browsed the shelves while listening to the owner in conversation with a charming elderly gentleman book collector who had come in asking, 'Could you direct me to your children's section, please? I'm looking for Ladybird Books, particularly early ones, with dust jackets.'

'You're unlikely to find any of those,' said the owner, rather discouragingly, I thought.

'Well, sometimes I do, every now and then, in charity shops, if I get lucky,' said the collector.

'Yes, well, you'd have to get very lucky.'

'Do you know that place in Harrogate, near the bus station? They've got a whole cabinetful.'

'Yes, well, you've got to be really lucky.'

'Hm. Do you know London? Do you know the Charing Cross book quarter? They have some there, but, oh, the prices!'

'Yes, well, that's London, isn't it?' the owner went on.

I left them to it and went into another room that had not been open the last time I had visited the shop. It had a slightly damp air. I found a Picador I had never seen before, Robert Edric's *In the Days of the American Museum*, and one I had bought at least twice before, Salman Rushdie's *Shame*, this one for its inclusion, a blank postcard of the West Terrace of Sandringham House. Also JM Coetzee's *The Life and Times of Michael K* (King Penguin), which had been recommended to me by a nice man I met at a wedding, and Ben Okri's *Songs of Enchantment* (Vintage), for its inclusion (a pressed poppy) and Celia Fremlin's *Appointment With Yesterday* (Gollancz), because she's brilliant. (I'm grateful to Blackwells bookseller Sarah Wenig for recommending her to me.) Some of these were unpriced, so I took them to the owner and asked him if the books in the other room, if they were unpriced, were a fixed price.

He said, 'If you show them to me, I'll tell you what the prices are.'

I handed them over and the ones I was only buying for their inclusions turned out to be £3 each, not extortionate prices, but the books carried an air of dampness and I couldn't help feeling that their prices should have been written in, allowing me to make informed choices.

I hesitated and he leaned forward across the desk and implored, 'Oh, please buy these! Because some people, you know, they come in, they talk to you for half an hour and they have a browse and then they don't buy anything. I had a fellow in earlier, talked to me for half an hour and then he didn't buy anything. He was looking for Ladybird Books and I showed him one. It was just what he wanted, but he said it wasn't in good enough condition.'

Whether this was right or not, it felt wrong.

Still, I had found a new Celia Fremlin, which I will definitely read, and I still intend to try the Coetzee, even though I didn't get on with his *Waiting For the Barbarians*. The Okri will join my very small sub-collection of books containing pressed flowers (a four-leaf clover in a Livre de Poche edition of Aragon's *Le paysan de Paris* and a red carnation in a Pan paperback of David Ambrose's *Superstition*) and the Rushdie, with its blank postcard, will be good for workshops. (Take along a bunch of books with blank postcard inclusions and hand them out and ask people to write something inspired by the combination of the book and the postcard, then let them keep the book – and the postcard.) I wonder what I prefer: blank postcards or postcards that have been written on and sent (or not sent)? It depends. I like the postcard I found at page 67 of a long and apparently unfinished (in the sense of unread) novel by a highly regarded but somewhat divisive British writer whose every public utterance I find profoundly objectionable. The postcard is written by an American woman, or a woman living in or visiting America, and was sent to a literary agent based in London, who then used it as a bookmark, but she appears not to have got beyond page 67, making this copy of this novel an unread book as far as she was concerned, while it would already have been an unread book for me, because of who it's by and how long it is (over 500 pages).

An old friend used not to read new novels by Stephen King despite the fact that King was his favourite writer. Or, to be more accurate, precisely because King was his favourite writer. The fact was that my friend loved King's early novels so much, he couldn't bear the thought that he might find himself at some point reading a new King novel and feeling that it wasn't quite as good as *The Shining* or *The Stand*. And so he stopped reading his favourite writer, apart from occasionally going back and re-reading the early ones.

I used to tell my friend I couldn't understand this, but, if I think about my favourite writer, Derek Marlowe, I am reminded that I haven't actually read Marlowe's last two novels, *The Rich Boy From Chicago* and *Nancy Astor*, partly for the same reason and partly because I'm saving them up, because I know there will not be any more, since Marlowe died in 1996. We never met, but had had a plan to meet in 1995. I waited in the bar at the Kensington Hilton for an hour before calling the number where Marlowe was staying in London. In those days he lived in Los Angeles and made infrequent visits to the UK. Marlowe answered. He had forgotten our meeting and was extremely apologetic. It was now too late – he had a full diary – and he was flying back the following day. He promised that when he next came to London, we would go out for dinner, to the restaurant of my choice. He later wrote to apologise again and to put his promise in writing, adding that leaving me waiting at the Hilton bar was not something he would wish on anyone. In 1996, however, he became ill and on 14 November he died.

One sees Marlowe's novels occasionally in second-hand bookshops. There have been recent print editions from Silvertail Books of *A Dandy in Aspic* and *Memoirs of a Venus Lackey*, but the former, at least, was spoiled by typesetting and production errors. I didn't see a copy of the latter. These titles and *Nightshade* and *Somebody's Sister* appear to be available in Kindle editions from Silvertail, but I have an idea what Marlowe would have thought of Kindles and e-books. He was an aesthete, a dandy; he loved the good things in life. No disrespect to Silvertail Books, but Marlowe's novels should be in print with Penguin Modern Classics (eight of his nine novels appeared as Penguins during his lifetime).

A tenth novel, working title *Black and White*, was left unfinished at Marlowe's death. The author's son, Ben, gave permission for the prologue and first two chapters to be published in *Neonlit: Time Out Book of New Writing Vol 1* (Quartet). Beyond that, Derek Marlowe's *Black and White* seems destined to remain an unread book.

Thursday 14 May 2009
Following a middle-aged woman up a staircase in a building that is either a second-hand bookshop or a house full of books. On the landing, one of her red shoes comes off.

In September 2023, I found a copy of my own *First Novel* (Vintage) in the Cancer Research charity shop in Didsbury, Manchester. The former owner had written his or her name and a date in pencil on the inside front cover and then scribbled over it in black pen before giving the book away, but if you hold it at an acute angle in low-angled winter sunlight, you can easily read the name and the date, which is given as 'February 22nd, 2014'. I'll shorten the name to P.

P has filled the book with underlinings, in pencil. All local street names are underlined. Also names of shops, businesses and retail parks. Towns, near and far. Some, but not all, of the books that are mentioned. Important plot points are underlined, but so are random exchanges of dialogue. Sometimes an underlining will be accompanied by an exclamation mark in the margin, occasionally a question mark instead. For instance, where I write, 'When the conditions were right – and they usually were between June and March, outside the rainy season . . .' there's an underlining of 'June and March' and a question mark in the margin. I can see how this might be puzzling, while technically correct (the long rains, in Zanzibar, fall in April and May), so I could have done a better job. Where Dr Shipman makes an appearance, unnamed, P has named him in the margin (with a big exclamation mark), but I don't know if P recognised him from the description or went back and made the note only after reading Shipman's name when it appears two pages later.

On the title page of the book, where, under the title, it says, 'A Mystery,' P has added, 'Too true!' And following the final words on the last page of the novel, P has written a single word: 'Good.' It's unclear whether this is a mark of approval of the narrator's actions at that crucial point or a comment on the novel as a whole, but I suspect the former, while not ruling out the possibility that it was an expression of relief at having got to the end.

It's not my favourite annotated second-hand copy of one of my own books – that's a copy of my novel *The Director's Cut* previously owned by film director Nicolas Roeg, discussion of which would fall outside the remit of this chapter – but it comes a close second.

5

Getting off at Stoke

A Wednesday in August, 2017. I get off the London Midland train at Stoke-on-Trent and walk down Church Street to check out the charity shops there. I buy Geoff Nicholson's *Day Trips to the Desert* (Sceptre) from the Samaritans for 30p and then walk up the hill (and down the hill) to Newcastle-under-Lyme. It's further than I thought and when I'm still some way short of the Oxfam shop I realise I'm going to be in danger of missing my Cross Country train to Stockport. Do I turn back or go on?

Getting off at Stoke (reminiscent of 'getting off at Haymarket', but I promise you it's nothing like that) was a way to cut down on rail fares, which, under Virgin, had risen and risen and continued to rise. (How we would long for Virgin, however, once Avanti West Coast took over the franchise.) You got London Midland from Euston to Stoke, then either Cross Country or, if the finances were over-stretched or you were feeling hardcore, Northern from Stoke to Stockport. To get the fares down to the absolute minimum, you booked advance tickets, so that you were tied to particular trains, which introduced a level of inconvenience, but brought with it opportunities: the hour you had to spend at Stoke could be spent either pretending to write in the Gourmet café on the station or heading out in search of second-hand books.

I go on. There's nothing in the Oxfam or the Cancer Research shop and I now have to get a move on. Do I stop for a bus or leg it? I leg it. I make it back to the station with minutes to spare. On arrival at Stockport, I walk home along the River Mersey to find a book waiting for me in the mail, a gift from Emma Towns-hend, who I know only as a lively and entertaining presence on social media. She has very kindly sent me a Penguin edition of Brigid Brophy's 1969 novel *In Transit*. It is in good condition with a cover illustrated by Allen Jones and contains a couple of inclu-sions: at page 45, a home-made cut-out yellow paper arrow, of uncertain purpose, and at page 145, a bookmark publicising the *Penguin Modern Stories* series, which at that point had reached its ninth volume. This dates the bookmark to 1971, also the year *In Transit* appeared in Penguin, so it's not unreasonable to assume the bookmark has been resting within its pages for 46 years.

Penguin Modern Stories was an anthology series published quarterly between 1969 and 1972 and concluding after twelve volumes, each one containing new short stories by a mixture of well-known authors and new writers. In most cases there were four contributors per volume, while three volumes showcased only three authors, and one volume made room for five. The editor was Judith Burnley, who had been Fiction Editor for *Woman's Own* and became Editorial Fiction Director at Penguin. The design, by David Pelham, featured a different solid colour for each volume – in order: red, green, yellow, brown, magenta, vermilion, indigo, teal, bright yellow, pink – across front and back covers and spine, with text in white and black, and large, striking, white numerals on front and back, which, in the cases of volumes ten and twelve, bled off the edge of the cover, perhaps suggesting the series had not been expected to reach double figures. Arguably, however, these are the most striking-looking volumes in the series, precisely because of the bleed.

A box set containing volumes one to six was issued in 1970. I found one of these box sets in Oxfam Bookshop Bloomsbury Street in May 2023 and couldn't resist its £15 price tag, even though I already had one, bought second-hand before I started keeping a record of these things. At page 51 in volume six, in the box set, the first page of Dan Jacobsons's second story, I found a corner torn from a page of the *Radio Times*, a fragment of radio listings from an unknown moment in time. From 8.32 until 9.55 the offerings being broadcast on the featured station – Radio 2, I'm guessing – would be 'as Radio 1', then, at 9.55, came *For Younger Listeners*, featuring 'The Jumble', by Margaret Bentley.

On the day I broke my journey in Stoke and came home to find Brigid Brophy's *In Transit* with its *Penguin Modern Stories* bookmark, I already owned not only a box set containing volumes one to six, but also a complete set of the series acquired gradually over the last three decades. On 23 October 2018, in Oxfam Books & Music Islington, I spotted the yellow spine of volume four of the series among the offerings on the short stories shelves and thought it would be a nice thing to start collecting a second set. Maybe they would make a good present, I thought.

Hm, maybe.

Over the next few months, then, I set about acquiring a second set. I knew I could go online and achieve that in an afternoon, but where's the fun in that? Instead, it was simply a question of looking out for those telltale coloured spines in any charity shops and second-hand bookshops I happened to be in. The randomness of it, the aleatory nature of the process, appeals.

I like new bookshops, but I *love* second-hand bookshops, and not just because the books I tend to be after, or the editions I'm after them in, are not in print. I like *not* knowing what I'm going to come across, just as I like not knowing what birds I might see on a walk over the moors, or what lost items I might find on a walk through any town or city.

I find *Penguin Modern Stories 5* in Book & Comic Exchange, or whatever it's called that week, unless it's just my imagination that the veteran second-hand shop in Notting Hill is constantly changing its name. *Penguin Modern Stories 3* in Oxfam Bookshop Coventry. *Penguin Modern Stories 2* in Gosford Books, Coventry. *Penguin Modern Stories 3* in Oxfam Books & Music Islington. *Penguin Modern Stories 4* in Book & Record Bar, West Norwood. *Penguin Modern Stories 6*, *8* and *9* in the Skoob Books pop-up in the Brunswick Centre (where I'm also tempted by a copy of Alan Bold's *Picador Book of Erotic Prose* with an inscription from 'B' to 'Steve' wishing him a happy second anniversary – a temptation I resist because it's £5). *Penguin Modern Stories 11* in Oxfam Dalston.

Keen-eyed readers may have spotted that I now own three copies of *Penguin Modern Stories 3*. Sometimes you are forced to admit that the impulse to collect is stronger than the will. It takes over, trashing the motivation you believed was controlling it. So you come up with a new plan to retro-justify the continued collecting. In this case, wouldn't it be nice to collect one copy of volume one, two copies of volume two, three copies of volume three and so on up to twelve copies of volume twelve? Wouldn't that collection, when complete, make a satisfying photograph? A bit like my photograph – which I set up and my wife kindly took – of me sitting in the bath reading the Editions de Minuit Double edition of Jean-Philippe Toussaint's novel *La salle de bain*, the cover of which features a man sitting in a bath. It's not quite mise en abyme, or maybe it is? (I can't deny I was thrilled when Jean-Philippe Toussaint liked the photo on Instagram.)

If you had asked me at any point during the 1980s to name my favourite short story writer of all time, I would not have hesitated to name William Sansom, who Judith Burnley chose to lead the team out on to the pitch, as it were, an analogy that will seem somewhat random until we get around to Brian Glanville in *Penguin Modern Stories 10*.

Of Sansom's two stories in *Penguin Modern Stories 1,* I prefer the first one, 'Down at the Hydro', in which a retired colonel has booked a few days at a spa. He is attracted to a guest, Mrs Mackay, who is married but is also attracted to him. They tentatively approach and withdraw and something happens that could develop, but then her husband arrives. The second story, 'The Marmalade Bird', in which a husband and wife peck at each other on holiday in Morocco is less effective, but beautifully written, because Sansom never wrote badly.

Jean Rhys's 'I Spy a Stranger' is a formally inventive tale about war, gossips and mental illness, while 'Temps Perdi' is a most singular story, although one broken down into numbered sections. A house, 'Rolvenden', on the east coast of England, is described in detail, lending it the status of a character. At the bottom of the third page of the story in the copy in which I read it there is a stamp identifying the book as the property of Fairfax School, Lister Avenue, Bradford 4. Just a couple of paragraphs later, the coalmen arrive.

> The clatter of coal on zinc. Then a man's voice said, 'That's the bathroom.'

'Well what about it? Why are you looking at it? Is there a woman in the ditch?' said a second voice.

'Why d'you think I'd look at her if there was?' the first voice said, very offended. 'Why should you think I'd look at a blank, blank cow in a blank, blank, blank ditch?'

The narrator is overhearing the conversation, from inside the kitchen, the coalmen being outside. Are the blanks words she can't hear? Or are they foul language the narrator is choosing not to hear, as it were? Or choosing – as if she knew the book was going to be handed out to pupils at Fairfax School, Lister Avenue, Bradford 4 – to censor to protect innocent minds?

Before we really know what's going on, the story has progressed to its second part, headed 'The Sword Dance and the Love Dance'. We seem to be in Vienna now, between the wars, but there are Japanese officers and the French, Germans and English are present also or at least spoken about. Part three, 'Carib Quarter', takes us to the island of Dominica. 'The night in Temps Perdi is full of things chirping and fluttering.' A greater contrast with the east coast of England is hard to imagine.

This is a story that would repay hours of deep reading and research. Indeed, a quick look online offers you a glimpse of numerous academic papers tucked away in various hiding places.

In 1975, David Plante would be included in Giles Gordon's anthology *Beyond the Words: Eleven Writers in Search of a New Fiction*, which I bought from Oxfam's Colne Road shop in Huddersfield in December 2018 along with an exciting job lot of BS Johnson first editions. Contributors were invited to preface their story with a note. Plante offered his in the form of a letter to Gordon. In it he wrote, 'It is what is left out of writing, what writing can't state, which possesses me – certain senses, certain states of consciousness, as real to us as eating and sleeping and working.' His stories in *Penguin Modern Stories 1* explore themes of death, grief, suicide and human contact. His work is often surprising, in both content and approach.

Much as I love Sansom's work and admire the stories of Rhys and Plante, my favourite story in the book is the shortest one, by Bernard Malamud, 'My Son the Murderer', which comes last and in which you're never quite sure what is a thought and what is a line of dialogue and who has spoken or thought which one. It's disorienting and very effective.

Since I mentioned *Penguin Modern Stories 10* and because I don't intend to consider the twelve volumes in numerical order, let's have a little look at the only volume in the series that manages to squeeze in five authors, namely Brian Glanville, Janice Elliott, Jennifer Dawson, Paul Winstanley and Jean Stubbs. I wouldn't have wanted to see any of these names left out, although one can imagine a version of this book in which Glanville's contribution takes up less space and all the other writers are offered more. Maybe a second or different Jennifer Dawson story would have been more fun, or maybe I just struggle with stories about religious orders. I had enjoyed Dawson's first novel, *The Ha-Ha*, which I found in a lovely Panther edition in the All Aboard charity shop in West Hampstead. The novel's main character, Josephine, is a patient in an asylum who goes to work for an elderly couple categorising their library. She likes to explore the asylum grounds and likes to sit in the grass beyond the ha-ha, which is where she meets Patrick from the male asylum. 'The Adventuress', however, in *Penguin Modern Stories 10*, does not make me want to rush out and find more of her stories, if indeed there are any more. There's clearly no shortage of Brian

Glanville stories. His lengthy biographical note reveals that he had published three collections before his inclusion in *Penguin Modern Stories 10*, to which he contributes four stories, one about a man wanting to leave his wife for a younger woman, one about a young woman trying to choose between her American boyfriend and her Italian lover, one about a female English Olympic athlete falling for the charms of a Uruguayan wrestler and finally, the only one I really liked, about the England football team's mascot. Glanville's note also claims that he wrote the first serious fiction about professional football to be published in the UK, which got me checking my bookshelves for my Stan Barstow collections. The Yorkshire writer's first collection, *The Desperadoes*, was published, like Glanville's short fiction debut, *A Bad Streak*, in 1961.

I like Janice Elliott and the story of hers I liked best was 'The Noise From the Zoo', which I read walking along the Regent's Canal past London Zoo, from which direction I did hear a variety of noises, which definitely added to the experience. Two single stories, by Paul Winstanley and Jean Stubbs, respectively, complete the volume and are the two stories I like best, particularly the Winstanley.

Saturday 21 January 2023
Mind, Kingsland Road, Dalston, London.
Young couple, taking up a lot of space.
Her: Lots of Ian McEwan.
Him: [. . .]
Her: Anything?
[Long pause.]
Him: Nah.

In June 2023, I take the train to Glossop. In the Oxfam they have a copy of the Granada paperback of JG Ballard's *Low-flying Aircraft* that I spent months tracking down in the 1980s, somehow ending up with two copies. I say 'somehow' but I think I understand how this happens. You look for a book for so long that, even once you find it, the desire to carry on looking for it doesn't get switched off. It's become a habit. So, when you find a second copy, even though you know you've already got it, you may end up buying it.

A Nightjar reader in the US tells me in an email how he has 'somehow' . . . 'accidentally' . . . become a collector of small press publications. 'For example,' he says, 'I now own all but three first edition titles from Egaeus Press.' (Egaeus Press books are undeniably lovely.) He adds, in brackets, 'I hope it goes without saying that this email is just between you and me, and not to be forwarded to my wife by any means, because I'm sure you wouldn't want to see an immediate halt to my purchasing powers.'

Another reader, the presenter, writer and journalist Stephen Smith, who used to do the culture bits on *Newsnight* when *Newsnight* still had culture on it, hearing I was writing a follow-up to *White Spines*, wrote to say, 'One thing I hope you'll cover is how the people you share your homes with feel about all your books, and where you stash them. I'm reduced to smuggling books indoors past my long-suffering missus: *watch the wall, my darling, while the Thomas Manns go by.* New books are secreted like miniatures of gin or catholic priests.'

I checked with Stephen that he was happy for me not only to include his quote in this book, but to attribute it to him by name. He agreed on condition that I assure him the book would never be selected by his wife's reading group. I would like to assure him now that I am doing everything in my power to prevent that happening.

When my wife and I got together, we lived in different cities and preferred to keep both homes and go between the two. While this creates some difficulties – I'm not entitled to a 60+ Oyster card and she doesn't enjoy any concessionary fares in Manchester, but then come to think of it neither do I – it also means I can continue to pile books high in my Manchester flat, as long as I keep a path clear to the sofa. In my wife's London flat, however, where I respect and appreciate her opposition to clutter, I have started to make creative use of hidden spaces. It's not only jumpers that can be tidied away in drawers.

On a corner site down a side street off the other side of the High Street in Glossop is the fabulous George Street Books, a community bookshop, which I visited for the first time a year ago, finding a Picador I didn't have, Robert Edric's *The Earth Made of Glass*, as well as other Picadors with interesting features – interesting to me, that is – including Louis Begley's *Wartime Lies* previously owned by a Laurence Marks, William Styron's *Lie Down in Darkness* with a different cover, by George Underwood, from the one I had, and Alice Hoffman's *Turtle Moon* also with a different cover, by Elaine Cox.

All I can find in June 2023 is Geoffrey Household's *Arrows of Desire* (Penguin). Something about it, whether it's the blurb or the '80s cover, tells me it's unlikely to be as good as any the four Household novels I've read, which appeared in matching green spines and black covers and brightly coloured type on the Penguin Crime list in 1971. Reading Household for the first time – I read *Rogue Male* in September 2018, having bought it and *Watcher in the Shadows* from Oxfam Richmond on Thames – was a revelation. I couldn't believe it was written in

1939. It felt much less dated than Nigel Balchin's *The Small Back Room*, published four years later. The experience was a little like when I first read Raymond Chandler: I literally couldn't put it down, or I suppose I should say I literally did not want to put it down, but how else could I write down all of Household's great lines that I wanted to remember, like 'The sort of man whom one instantly accuses of any practical joke that has been played deserves whatever is coming to him' or 'It's easy to make a man confess the lies he tells to himself; it's far harder to make him confess the truth.' The same compulsion took hold of me when I read *A Rough Shoot*. (When I got *Rogue Male* and *Watcher in the Shadows* home from Richmond on Thames, I was pleased to find I already had a copy of *A Rough Shoot*, with an inclusion, a leaflet from the Kensington branch of the Leeds Building Society that looks like it dates from 1971.) It's lighter than *Rogue Male*, but largely set in the same Dorset countryside Household conjured up so vividly in the earlier novel. International politics and terror are again to the fore, but it's his prose that makes me a fan: '. . . I must have been nothing but a piece of night which moved.' *Watcher in the Shadows* is very similar – in a good way – to *Rogue Male* and *A Rough Shoot*. More beautifully written suspense-in-the-English-countryside, this time the Cotswolds. My copy was previously – perhaps originally – owned by S James, who added a date – 'Oct. '72'. (I bought a second copy of *A Rough Shoot*, with an inclusion in the form of a business card from Swiss Cottage Cars, from the Mind shop in East Finchley and sent it to my friend Ian Cunningham, who I met when we both worked at *Reader's Digest*. I published Ian's first short story in an anthology in 1992 and he's never written a word of fiction since, so I both launched and sank his career as a short story writer. He did, however, write *A Reader's*

Guide to Writers' London (Prion), for which I can take no credit whatsoever.)

I showed my Households to Matthew Adamson, a former MA student whose debut short story I published in the Nightjar anthology *The Invisible Collection*, and he kindly offered me another Household in the same series. He had bought *A Time to Kill* in Scotland while visiting bookshops on what he has called his White Spines Tour, in which he visits every bookshop mentioned in my earlier book. I couldn't have come up with a better way of informing booksellers that I have written about them than to have someone follow in my footsteps and tell them. I should really be paying him.

An ex-Fascist called Pink, a house-breaking scene in Dorset, a complicated story of spying on a man who is helping the Russians to create a biological weapon – it's all in *A Time to Kill*. An added bonus this time is that some of the action takes place at sea, on boats. Only in books is how I like to go to sea. So susceptible am I to motion sickness that even watching Polanski's *Knife in the Water* or Lars von Trier's *Breaking the Waves* has me reaching for the sick bucket. Actually, come to think of it, I remember feeling slightly queasy reading BS Johnson's *Trawl*, the avant garde British author's third novel about a three-week voyage on a deep-sea fishing trawler that he researched by undertaking a three-week voyage on a deep-sea fishing trawler.

BS Johnson is one of the featured authors in *Penguin Modern Stories 7*, which is the first volume in the series that I read from start to finish. It kicks off with a long story from Anthony Burgess about going back to Shakespeare's time to see if he wrote the plays credited to him. I find Susan Hill's second story, 'How Soon Can I Leave?', about a 'friendship' between

Miss Bartlett and Miss Roscommon, quite affecting. Miss Roscommon persuades Miss Bartlett to move in with her, but then controls her and belittles her. Miss Bartlett moves out, but her home is under threat from the sea and she eventually decides to move back in, but she leaves it a day too late. I struggle with the two longish stories by Yehuda Amichai. The BS Johnson stories come at the end of the book. They show their age in terms of their attitudes to women, or the first one does, 'Instructions For the Use of Women'. I don't get much out of 'For Bolocks Read Blocks Throughout'. Best, perhaps, is 'Mean Point of Impact', about an artillery offensive against the Cathedral of St Anselm.

Armed with my copy of Household's *Arrows of Desire* ('It is 700 years after the Age of Destruction and London is just a forest'), I take the footpath south out of Glossop, which leads me up a 45-degree hill that soon has me thinking of the video that plays in a loop in my GP surgery's waiting room. 'If you get out of breath doing something you used to be able to do,' says a friendly male voice, 'it could be a sign of lung disease, heart disease, or even cancer.' Cheers. Thanks very much. I may not be quoting verbatim, but short of making an appointment to see my GP, I'm not sure how else to check. The internet seems not to be familiar with this particular video. And making an appointment to see my GP – well, I'd have to log on before 7am, or is it telephone before 8am? Which is it this week?

Anyway, by the time I reach the top of the hill, it is pouring with rain. I follow the bridleway towards New Mills, confused by signs that suggest that access has been suspended while the evidence in front of me – a bridleway, gates that open and close – suggests otherwise. In the field to my left a familiar-looking bird rises at a low angle from the long grass and describes the diameter of a large semi-circle at the centre of which I remain, even as I move forward, like an advancing protractor. I'm not sure if that analogy works, or was worth the effort (I look up protractors to see if there's a technical word for that bit at the centre of the straight edge – there doesn't appear to be). The curlew's mournful, burbling cry confirms the bird's identification. It falls silent before it reaches the apex of its flight, allowing me to become aware of a parliament of bleating sheep over the next rise. The rain continues to fall, plastering my shirt to my body. I feel fabulously alive, in defiance of the shortness-of-breath video nasty.

Several miles later, my feet squelching in my supposedly waterproof shoes, I arrive in Mew Mills and Adam Morris, proprietor of High Street Books, is good enough not to object to the wet footprints as I make my way to his paperback fiction shelves. I am pleased to find duplicates of *Penguin Modern Stories 3* and *7*, a nice Penguin edition of *Lolita*, and copy of Andrea Ashworth's Picador title *Once in a House on Fire* containing a blank postcard from the Red Sea. I explain to Adam why I'm buying the Ashworth, since he knows about my Picador obsession. I can't possibly need it for the collection, as it's the second-most-often-found Picador after Graham Swift's *Last Orders* and I'm bound already to have it, which indeed I do. From under the counter he produces his box of inclusions, which he usually removes from books, he tells me. I do my best to conceal my horror. He sifts through his box and picks out a postcard. On the front is a green stamp to the value of one and a half old pence bearing the left profile of King George VI. Postmarked 5.45pm, 24 October 1951, the postcard is addressed to G Budd Esquire of 5 Rodger Street, Anstruther. On the reverse side of the card, which is printed with the name of

Crail Amateur Football Club, of 36 Nethergate, Crail, is a note to inform Mr Budd that he has been selected to play against St Monance FC that coming Saturday, kick off at 2.45pm. The card was posted on the Wednesday. Mr Budd was advised to reply immediately in the event that he was unable to play, which wouldn't have given Crail's manager much time to find another player.

Adam kindly gives me the card and I tell him I'll keep it in *Lolita*, but now I'm thinking I might send it to Bread & Butter Café, present-day occupants of 5 Rodger Street, Anstruther. (I do this a few weeks later. I hope they received it. My experience of Royal Mail suggests I shouldn't assume they did.)

When I get around to reading *Penguin Modern Stories 3*, I enjoy the Philip Roth stories more than I expected to, especially the second one, 'An Actor's Life For Me', about a man who thinks his wife is watching the naked man in the apartment across the way. I feel I need to be careful regarding what I say about Margaret Drabble's short fiction since the appearance of her collected stories, *A Day in the Life of a Smiling Woman* (Penguin Modern Classics), in 2011, when editor José Francisco Fernández suggested in his introduction that Michael Moorcock and I had been wrong to describe Drabble's contribution to *Neonlit: Time Out Book of New Writing Volume 2* (Quartet), 'The Caves of God', as, respectively, 'a rarity' and 'a rare excursion into the short form'. I still think that thirteen short stories is a relatively low number in what was then a forty-five-year career, allowing one with some justification to get excited about publishing a new one, even if we were rescuing an old, unpublished story from oblivion. As Fernández pointed out, it had been written for a book about 'secrets' that never saw the light of day. Maybe around the time of 'Crossing the Alps'? Fernández did not say.

More recently, at least two further stories have been published, in Sarah Eyre and Ra Page's *The New Abject* and Catherine Taylor's *The Book of Sheffield* (both Comma Press).

One of my copies of *Penguin Modern Stories 3* was previously acquired in December 1970 by CD Hollis, who wrote his or her name, and that date, in black ink on the inside front cover using a fountain pen with an italic nib. I wonder what CD Hollis thought of the two very short Giles Gordon stories that bring *Penguin Modern Stories 3* to a close. I have read them before in Gordon's 1975 collection *Farewell Fond Dreams* and I love their invention and playfulness. I also enjoy the Jay Neugeboren stories: 'Finkel', about the widowed professor getting annoyed by the building super but coming round to him in the end; 'Joe', about a local man who shares his pornography with adolescent boys; and 'The Pass', about a boy in a psychiatric hospital who gets a day out at the beach with his parents that doesn't quite go to plan.

Following a trail from Giles Gordon to Robert Nye, since Gordon included Nye in his *Beyond the Words* anthology, I read *Penguin Modern Stories 6* next. The Robert Nye story is rather challenging and not very rewarding; it's in what I'm slowly realising is the experimental slot, the last position in the book. Gordon occupies this slot in volume three, BS Johnson in volume seven. The opening slot is generally reserved for the biggest name; in the case of volume six, this is Elizabeth Taylor. That name, in the context of Penguin paperbacks, says Muriel Spark's *The Driver's Seat* to me, with its cover image taken from the 1974 film directed by Giuseppi Patroni Griffi and starring Hollywood actress Elizabeth Taylor (1932–2011), so it's about time I acquaint myself with novelist and short story writer Elizabeth Taylor (1912–75). Her opening story is 'Sisters', in which the surviving sister of a highly regarded writer is visited by a 'hideously glinty young man', who is writing a book about the deceased sister. He looks at Mrs Mason, who has against her better judgment let him enter her home, in her 'silvery-grey wool dress', and sees 'an enormous salmon'. She even has, in his opinion, 'a salmon shape – thick from the shoulders down and tapering away to surprisingly tiny, out-turned feet. He imagined trying to land her.' Throughout the rest of the story he tries to do just this, but she manages to get rid of him. Later, she realises he got her to say things she regrets and that people will, as a result, be talking about her, which she had wanted to avoid. It's an excellent story that fills me with excitement for more of her work.

Elsewhere in volume six, I like Maggie Ross's story about a man who appears to have drowned his wife, but I fail to get on with Dan Jacobson.

The spines of two of my four copies of *Penguin Modern Stories 9* have faded from what I earlier described as teal to a shade of blue almost indistinguishable from that of *Penguin Modern Stories 2*. One of them was previously owned, as was one of my five copies of *Penguin Modern Stories 8*, by Sheelagh, who wrote 'Sheelagh 77' on the flyleaf of both books.

I only have two notes from my reading of *Penguin Modern Stories 9*. Firstly, an observation about telephone boxes in VS Pritchett's story 'The Editor Regrets . . .': 'They were always unpleasantly warmed by random emotions left behind in them.' Very true, I feel. The other was about a line in Ruth Fainlight's story 'The Expatriates'. She writes: '"Hello, Dick," Max called as he sighted him. "Here comes the manager," he grinned over his shoulder to Joe and Jeanette who were talking near the back of the bar.' When I was teaching creative writing I would advise students against using a non-speech verb to attribute dialogue, arguing that you can't giggle, sigh or, indeed, grin any actual words at all. But then my colleague, Joe, not the Joe in Ruth Fainlight's story, but my ex-colleague and very good friend Joe, said that I'm the most literal-minded person he knows. I wasn't sure what he meant by it at the time, but I have reflected on it and decided that I'm also the most literal-minded person *I* know. I'm not entirely sure it's a bad thing, but nor do I think that Joe necessarily thought it was either.

Notes aside, what I remember from *Penguin Modern Stories 9* is that I quite liked Frederick Busch's story about US Army call-up medical exams, but my favourite story in that volume was 'The Fifty Minute Hour' by Mel Calman, who was a cartoonist rather than a writer. Indeed, the second of his two contributions, which appear in the experimental slot, is a cartoon. The first of his pieces, 'The Fifty Minute Hour', is only two pages long, but is very powerful. I think it might be one of my favourite stories from the whole series. You could say, I suppose, that it's about grief and psychiatry. Or about the fear of death. Or maybe even about the dark attraction of death. 'It's better for you to be wheeled gently along on this black trolley than to struggle against the tide of your black fears.'

Penguin Modern Stories 8 has the fewest stories of any volume in the series, just five, from three writers: William Trevor, AL Barker and CJ Driver. I can't help wishing Judith Burnley had brought forward VS Pritchett from volume nine or hung on to BS Johnson from volume seven and swopped either of them in for William Trevor, not because I don't like Trevor, but just to have three writers in one volume all using a pair of initials. But then Trevor's stories are the highlights in volume eight.

Barker's 'Watch It', a gentle, touching ghost story, is the most effective of her three contributions, while CJ Driver's story, set mostly in South Africa, in which the narrator tells us about his friend Mike, a liberal, like the narrator, who gets involved in anti-authority activities, achieves considerable power towards the end of the story as the narrator speculates on what might have happened to Mike towards the end of his life. It's partly, I think, the fact that the narrator doesn't know what's happened to Mike, partly the fact he knows it's most likely that he's dead and yet can still imagine these different scenarios, because the desire for continuing life is so strong, and partly the fact of the story coming to its end, of which we are aware both because we can *feel* the end approaching and because we can see there are not many pages left.

Both of Trevor's stories are very good. In the second one, 'A Choice of Butchers', a little boy is puzzled by his father's antipathy to Henry, who comes to work for him in his butcher's shop. The man's visits to the boy's room are a comfort to the boy, who is upset after seeing his father kissing a young woman, not the boy's mother. What harm is there in a kiss on the top of his head? When Henry is asked to leave, the boy is upset and we feel sympathy for Henry, despite our suspicions, perhaps because beyond our suspicions we sense that Henry is managing, just about, to control his behaviour. As often with Trevor, even though these stories are on the long side, there's a lot left out. A number of writers have spoken or written wisely about the most important words being those not on the page. Trevor is the one I usually quote on this subject. Perhaps because he practises what he preaches and is such an effective practitioner. And, of course, now that I want to quote him on this subject, I can't find the quote.

On Monday 21 February, 2022, I walked from Stoke Newington down to the Regent's Canal, then west along the canal all the way to Golborne Road, in west London, via, first of all, Oxfam Books & Music Islington. I like the fact that, if you are walking along the canal from Hackney to Islington or beyond, when you reach Colebrooke Row you have to ascend to street level, because of the 960-yard-long Islington Tunnel built in 1818 by engineer James Morgan. Your best route to the western end of the tunnel, where you can rejoin the canal, takes you past Oxfam Books & Music Islington. I mean, it's perfect really.

There I bought Umberto Eco's *The Name of the Rose* (Picador) for its inclusion, a blank postcard of Memling's *The Annunciation* and an invitation to Mr Richard Baker from the Arms Control and Disarmament Department of the Foreign and Commonwealth Office, to a Christmas party on Wednesday 21 December (no year given) at 6pm in Room E 102. In the top right-hand corner of the invitation, written in pencil, are the words 'Yes please'.

At Portobello Road, in the Vision Foundation, I spent a slightly surprising £4 on Patrick Modiano's *In the Café of Lost Youth* (Maclehose), thinking it might be a good present for my brother-in-law, as it was in good nick and my brother-in-law might think I'd bought it new. At this point, if I were writing a text, I would insert a winking emoji.

My destination was Oxfam Bookshop Portobello, where, I had been advised by Charles Boyle, short story writer, author and publisher of CBeditions, I would find a stash of *Penguin Modern Stories*. All I could find was a white-spined Picador edition of Cormac McCarthy's *City of God* with a rogue design element on the spine, which would be a good addition to the anomalies section of my Picador collection. No *Penguin Modern Stories*.

Two months later found me back on Portobello Road and in the Oxfam Bookshop I found those copies of *Penguin Modern Stories 8* and 9, both inscribed 'Sheelagh 77' on the flyleaf. If these were part of the stash Charles had seen, why hadn't I spotted them two months earlier? And where were the rest of them? Two was hardly a stash. (I'm using the word 'stash', but I'm not saying Charles used it. Later, Charles kindly sent me a copy of the Picador Classics edition of Baudelaire's *Intimate Journals*, which he bought from the same Oxfam Bookshop.)

Throughout 2022 I suffered from intermittent shoulder pain. Actually, I didn't know whether to call it shoulder pain or back pain. When I was able to pinpoint it, the epicentre seemed to be in my back just to the right of my left shoulder blade, but, unhelpfully, it would move around. The phrase 'referred pain' comes to mind, but I don't really understand what is meant by it. My wife wondered if it was connected to the carrying around of heavy tote bags full of books. But I would usually carry such a bag on my right shoulder, I said. Maybe your left shoulder is compensating? Ah. Maybe you should use a rucksack? I was thinking I should go back to the physio who I had seen for my shoulder injury related to vaccine administration (SIRVA). Or see an osteopath.

In January 2023 I read a news story about an individual who had died of bile duct cancer. I hadn't even known you could get bile duct cancer. He'd had shoulder pain. It had been so bad it had woken him up in the night. Mine hadn't been that bad, but that didn't matter. *Hi, my name is Shoulder Pain. I'll be your possible symptom of bile duct cancer.*

Driving between London and Manchester, I stopped off in Bedford. The Eagle Bookshop is always worth a visit. I found a few things: Lionel Davidson's *Smith's Gazelle* (Arrow) with a boarding pass in the name of Mr D Smith flying from London to Istanbul on Turkish Airlines. Another boarding pass in the same name, going from Heathrow to Newark on Virgin Atlantic, in a copy of Shane Moloney's *The Brush-Off* (Canongate). Normally, I would withhold the name, but Mr D Smith? In a book called *Smith's Gazelle*? Also: PM Hubbard's *The Holm Oaks* (Panther) with a British United passenger ticket, dated 1967, in the name of, I think (it was hard to read), Mr and Mrs Biggs, flying from Gatwick to Alderney. This got me excitedly Googling the timeline of Ronnie Biggs, but my excitement didn't last long. Also: a paperback copy of George MacBeth's *The Transformation* (Quartet), which meant I could give away my hardback. And finally, Cyril: a different Panther edition from the one I already have of John McGahern's *The Dark*, this one with a book plate in the name of Tom Youd and an address in Huntingdon. And finally, Esther: a copy of *Penguin Modern Stories 5*.

I've actually got six copies of *Penguin Modern Stories 5*, excluding the two copies in the two box sets. Only one of them has any distinguishing features. They are: a name and date in black fibre tip on the inside front cover, 'J Jenner. London. 1972'; and, at page 103, a bit of cardboard from a packet of blue Rizlas. I'm not saying the book didn't have other owners between J Jenner and me. It's quite likely that it did. But I regard the location of the Rizla packaging as significant, as page 103 marks the start of Andrew Travers' contribution to the volume, which takes the form of two stories, 'Babyface' and 'Don't Shoot'. These are, by some distance, my favourite stories in volume five.

I couldn't get into Penelope Gilliatt's four very different stories (one being a playscript). They don't convince me as worlds you can enter, as a reader. I like Benedict Kiely's story; his prose is a real pleasure. You can hear the writer's Irish voice and the characters dance into existence on the page. Anthony Burton's two stories, in the last position in the book, are disappointing – a frivolous story about an alien craft that lands in a field and the impact of its occupant on village life, and another, again rather frivolous, story about running for a train.

Andrew Travers' stories are darker and more experimental. 'Babyface' starts with the narrator inserting his key in his wife's front door. Instantly, the reader has questions. Travers uses a lot of brackets, probably too many, in what may be too earnest a striving for effect, but I don't mind that. He has some great images, for example, '(The revving of a lorry drives through the room dragging its load of noise through a thousand furnished rooms.)' In 'Don't Shoot', a man is flying over London, coming in to Heathrow. On arrival, he will check into an Earls Court hotel and enter room 28, where he will look under the bed. There he will find 'A tampax, a wire coat-hanger, five cigarette ends, a left gymshoe'. Travers is very good at describing the perception of sound. Another example: ' . . . they will enter the foyer below me, their normal voices will pour into my room through the window and also up the stairs along the corridor and under the door'.

The editor's note on Travers tells us he was born near Manchester in 1944. His two stories in *Penguin Modern Stories 5* were his first appearance in print and he was working on a novel called *Millionaire*. I can't find any record of such a novel ever being published, but I have found another story by Andrew Travers among my books. 'Drug Story' appears in the science fiction anthology *Science Against Man* edited by Anthony Cheetham. It looks like the anthology was published by Avon in the US in 1970, then by Macdonald in the UK in 1971, with my Sphere paperback following in 1972. Frustratingly, the Andrew Travers story, which is the last story in the book, is the only one not to be preceded by a note from the editor introducing the story. I am going to read it now.

The results of that reading are in and they are inconclusive. Could be the same Andrew Travers, but equally might not be. There are two examples of parentheses, both pretty standard usage. Possibly, if it was the same Andrew Travers and he knew he was writing a science fiction story, he thought a different style was called for. The story is about a prisoner in a gaol where individual cells can be picked up and moved and put back on their side, for the purpose of disturbance and disorientation. Sometimes the prisoner is free to go, but it seems he never gets very far before stumbling into more traps – or before he undergoes metamorphosis into a worm.

I enjoyed it, but not as much as the two stories in *Penguin Modern Stories 5*.

The first contributor to *Penguin Modern Stories 11* had a strong interest in science fiction. Kingsley Amis edited an anthology, *The Golden Age of Science Fiction*, and co-edited a series of SF anthologies with Robert Conquest, and was the author of a non-fiction work, *New Maps of Hell: A Survey of Science Fiction*. The first of Amis's two stories in *Penguin Modern Stories 11* is a science fiction story, but it's less interesting and original than the one by Andrew Travers – whether it's the same Andrew Travers or not, it's still by Andrew Travers – in *Science Against Man*. Amis's second story is a long one, sixty pages long, about a depressed poet who doesn't think he's any good.

I was reading it while walking in Batley in West Yorkshire. I had driven to Cleckheaton Library to meet author Amanda Huggins so she could sign copies of her Nightjar story, 'Signals'.

It was one of the last times I would do this, having decided that driving long distances to get boxes of chapbooks signed, when one considered the climate crisis, was unjustifiable.

Cleckheaton Library is wonderful. While Amanda signed her name 200 times and told me lots of funny stories, doing voices and everything, two library users strummed ukuleles at a neighbouring table. It could almost have been a spectator event. Leaving Amanda, I drove to Batley, as some casual online research had suggested there might be a second-hand bookshop there as well as a branch of Oxfam. I don't quite know how I formed the impression that Book Depot was a second-hand bookshop with lots of stock, because when I got to the Mill Outlet and Garden Centre, I could only see a branch of remainder shop chain The Works. I wandered around the Mill, which was weirdly interesting mainly because it was so empty and the few shoppers who were there were all older than me and these days that's saying something. Eventually I went in The Works and asked about Book Depot and it turned out Book Depot was the old name of The Works, or had been there before The Works, or something. So I set off, reading *Penguin Modern Stories 11*, to look for the large Oxfam I'd also found on the internet. It was a bright, sunny, autumn day. The Oxfam turned out to be a warehouse you couldn't enter without an appointment and there were no books there anyway, apart from the ones holding up a glass table in the reception area. So I headed back towards where I had parked the car, still reading, and on Grange Road I saw a middle-aged blonde woman with a brown dachshund coming towards me. She clocked the book and said, 'It must be good.' To be honest, I didn't know what to say to that, because I was half way through the second of the Amis stories and I wasn't enjoying it and didn't think it was very good at all.

Suddenly, the woman gasped. 'Eleven,' she said. 'Eleven eleven.'

The way I was holding the book allowed her to see front and back covers simultaneously. Two elevens.

'Yes,' I said.

She explained that eleven was her spirit number.

'Oh,' I said.

'Yes,' she said, adding that she was going to get the number tattooed.

'Where?' I asked.

'Here,' she said, showing me her wrist. She asked about the book. I showed it to her, explaining that it was a book of stories by three writers. She said, 'What's the story about that you're reading now?'

I said it was about a poet who had deliberately written some bad poetry to expose the flatterers who continued to insist on his genius.

Looking at me frankly, she said, 'You look spiritual.'

'Oh, no, not really,' I said. 'I'm not religious.'

She said, 'No, no, not me either, but I'm my own god. This is my god.' She gestured to the world around us. She said, 'I was in a dark place last year, but I haven't touched alcohol for fourteen months and I haven't smoked since January. I took up running.'

'That's great,' I said, 'and you're walking the dog. I walk a lot,' I added. 'I walk ten miles a day.'

She said she tries to get up to ten miles a day. I introduced myself and asked her her name and she said it was Joanne. I asked her if I could put her in my book and she said yes. She said that she had been in Tesco the day before and had put the divider on the conveyor and said to the man next to her in the queue, 'Unless you want to pay for mine,' and the man said yes and she said she was only joking. "'I've got money," and the man said, "No, I'd like to pay for your shopping,'" so she accepted.

After leaving Joanne I found a penny and it occurred to me that I find pennies more often than other coins. Do people drop more pennies than other coins, or do they just not bother to pick them up?

After leaving Batley I drove to Holmfirth where I visited the Oxfam Books & Music and bought MR James's *Ghost Stories of an Antiquary* (Penguin), a lovely edition with a grey, orange and black cover that would match my copy of William Sansom's *Selected Short Stories*, then I drove over Black Hill, which looked fantastic in the afternoon sunshine, to Glossop and George Street Books, where I had a lovely conversation with volunteer Sophie Pattinson, who said she had read *White Spines*. I bought a copy of Paul Auster's *A New York Trilogy*, with an ex-libris stamp in it, and, to give as presents, two gorgeous London Panther editions of Saki's short stories.

It was a great day.

Following Amis in *Penguin Modern Stories 11* are two finely written stories by R Prawer Jhabvala and two stories by New York-born David Zane Mairowitz. In 'The Police', a policeman is obliged to observe the punishment of a woman who has transgressed the law. As part of the observation, the policeman is required to participate in an act of intimacy with the offender. Or you might say the offender is forced to submit to a personal assault by the policeman.

I'm not sure I could tell you what Mairowitz's other story, 'The Grace', is about, but it contains lines like 'Between her legs a ravaged city is undergoing a post-war experience' and 'She comes upon a lake and swims in it naked to limber her body and, on its banks, she performs her ballet lessons, thrusting her legs to the air in postures of angular composure'.

I would be very interested to know what either R Aptaker or Elizabeth Fletcher made of Mairowitz's stories. R Aptaker wrote his or her name in block capitals on the inside back cover of one of my two copies of *Penguin Modern Stories 11* and Elizabeth Fletcher wrote her name and two addresses and phone numbers on the inside front cover of the other, adding a charming line drawing of two fishes swimming in an ornate pool. One of those addresses is a Grade II* listed manor house in Norfolk, the other a semi-detached house in Notting Hill that, according to the internet, was sold in 2023 for an eye-watering £28 million.

I make an appointment to see an osteopath recommended to me by the short story writer and children's author Cliff McNish. While I'm waiting for the appointment to come around, the pain in my shoulder seems to recede. I mention this to the osteopath when I turn up for the appointment at his consulting room in Peckham. 'Yes,' he says. 'That often happens. Now, if you could just jump up here and lie face down.'

After the appointment, I walk to Oxfam Bookshop Herne Hill, local branch of my ex-*Time Out* colleague and *I Told You I Was Ill* author John O'Connell, where I find duplicate copies of *Penguin Modern Stories 5* and *12*. I start reading *Penguin Modern Stories 12* and am pleased to find the pattern of not especially enjoying the work of whichever writer is deemed the most notable and given the opening slot not repeating itself. Olivia Manning's 'Ladies Without Escort' is an excellent read, as poignant and evocative as it is funny. Pam and Brenda, middle-aged women who become friends after both being voted on to the Pets' Club bazaar committee, go on a cruise together – on a working vessel rather than a ship designed for the purpose. They soon become targets for fellow passengers Karl – 'he had a worn, dried-out appearance as though pervaded through and through by the enervating fungus of failure' – and Leon – 'In spite of a long, dark-coloured nose and a loose mouth in which the teeth were as haphazard as the teeth of a rhino, he looked excessively pleased with himself' – who believe that because the ladies are 'without escort', their wishes must align with their own.

Something prevents me from fully engaging with Francis King's stories. Perhaps it's the anticipation I feel for those of Gabriel Josipovici, whose name, rightly or wrongly, one associates with the avant garde. 'Mobius the Stripper', divides the page into a top half and a bottom half and twin narratives about the artiste of the title mimic the two sides of a Möbius strip. I derived more pleasure from the subtler twists of 'The Agent', in which a spy bickers with his contact and endures the tedium of his job: 'It's the empty hours, he thought, when you have nothing to do, those are the worst.' His final story, 'The Voices', is an exercise in non-sequiturs and unfinished

Ian Cochrane's two stories, which round out the series, are more conventional, in an Irish tradition, than Josipovici's, leaving the reader to wonder why they have been placed in the experimental slot.

Nadine Gordimer is Geoff Dyer's favourite writer, according to his great joke at JM Coetzee's expense that I included in *White Spines* (and which you can easily find on YouTube), but on the strength of her two stories in *Penguin Modern Stories 4* she's unlikely to become mine. As Dyer points out, however, she won dozens of major awards, including the Booker Prize and the Nobel Prize, so only an idiot would discount her contribution to literature after reading a couple of short stories. I may be an idiot, but I am not discounting Nadine Gordimer's contribution to literature. Nor am I discounting those of Sean O'Faolain, or Shiva Naipaul, whose stories in *Penguin Modern Stories 4* mark his first appearance in print, if I say that once again it's the last author in the volume whose work I find most interesting. Isaac Babel's story about the creative process, 'Inspiration', is only three pages long, but in those three pages I feel I'm taken somewhere – to a town early in the morning, 'cold and blue, ghostly and gentle' – and that a small part of me stays there.

Blue is the colour of *Penguin Modern Stories 2*, featuring John Updike, Sylvia Plath and Emanuel Litvinoff. On one of my copies another name, Innes, has been added in blue ball-point at the top of that list on the cover. Why did I leave this volume until last to read? Maybe I thought John Updike would be boring or overly serious, or overly sure of his pre-eminence, and that this would come through in the work. His first story is fifty pages long and could have been told in half that. It's about a young couple who are cheating on their partners. They are trying to get back to their respective homes, by plane, after she joined him on a work trip. 'Bech in Romania' reads like an extended dream and feels like it might be based on the author's experience of being a visiting author in that country. And why not? I enjoyed it. The Plath story is good, about a young woman watching someone get a tattoo, if not quite displaying the free-wheeling narrative ebullience of her 'Johnny Panic and the Bible of Dreams' in the Picador anthology *The Naked i* edited by Frederick R Karl and Leo Hamalian. The Litvinoff stories, clearly partly autobiographical, are fascinating; I was struck by how the experience of being an adolescent male in an East End Jewish context in between the wars was remarkably similar to that of an adolescent male in south Manchester in the 1970s.

Litvinoff died in 2011. His obituary in the *Guardian* was written by Judith Burnley and includes these lines: 'I met Emanuel in 1955 and was involved with all of his work from then onwards. The stories that make up *Journey Through a Small Planet* were found by me at the back of drawers and in waste-paper baskets. Three of them were published in *Penguin Modern Stories 2* (1969), which I edited. They were then arranged in chronological order to create the autobiographical line for the book. I was particularly happy when the book was reprinted as a Penguin Modern Classic in 2008.'

A Wednesday in January, 2024. I'm back at Stoke-on-Trent changing trains on my way to Manchester. Nowadays, the money-saving route involves booking an advance from Euston to Stoke on London Northwestern, but changing at Stafford. You still have just under an hour at Stoke before the next Northern service, but you no longer have to leave the station in search of second-hand books, as there's a small selection in the back of the Gourmet café. Rather annoyingly, even if you buy a coffee, you're not allowed to pass beyond the barrier separating the platform side of the café from the street side, but there's nothing to prevent you from leaving the station and entering the café from the street – as long as the barista agrees to open the street door, which seems to need to be opened from the inside.

If I see bookshelves, I can be quite determined.

I pick out a cloth-bound hardback, *On Railways: At Home and Abroad* (Spring Books) by P Ransome-Wallis, with a foreword by Cecil J Allen and an ambiguous inscription, unsigned, in black ink on the flyleaf: 'To Ted, who revealed his interest at dinner, 8th Feb 63.'

6

Books in films

Leo Robson, in the *Guardian*, likened Scarlett Johansson's fabulously blank face in *Under the Skin* (2014) to a 'closed book'. The only book we see in Jonathan Glazer's film, an adaptation of Michel Faber's first novel, is an open book. When the mysterious male motorcyclist tidies up after Johansson's killing of the Good Samaritan swimmer from the Czech Republic, he unzips the swimmer's tent to reveal a book he had been in the middle of reading. The book is a hardback, lying open, but we never see its cover or get a close enough look at the text to see even if it is in English or Czech. The motorcyclist gathers it up along with everything else and we never see it again.

The book was the last book the swimmer from the Czech Republic ever read, albeit one he never got to finish. In Park Chan-wook's *Sympathy For Mr Vengeance* (2002), pre-cursor to the better-known *Oldboy* (2003), a young man, Ryu, tries to sell his kidney to obtain another kidney for his sister, but he is tricked by criminals, so takes revenge, but not until after, with the help of his terrorist girlfriend, Yeong-mi, he has kidnapped the daughter of his former employer, hoping to use the ransom money to pay for a kidney for his sister. Alone one day, Yeong-mi is reading a book when the doorbell goes. We don't know what the book is, but we know it's the last one she will ever read, because at the door is the father of the kidnapped child – and he has not come to discuss literature.

Books in films are often just books; we don't get to find out what they are. It's not important. What *is* important, though, sometimes, is that they're first editions. In M Night Shyamalan's *The Sixth Sense* (1999), Bruce Willis's wife gives her new man a book. We don't know what it is, only that it's a first edition, because she tells him.

In *Shadows in the Sun* (2009), directed by David Rocksavage, Robert (James Wilby) arrives at the home of his elderly mother, Hannah, and is a little put out to find a young man, Joe (Jamie Dornan), looking after Hannah. They read poetry to each other and share joints. Sounds like hell to me, but both activities seem to help ease the symptoms of Hannah's unspecified chronic condition. Still, Robert doesn't like the arrangement and nor does he like the fact that his mother has sold his late father's collection of first editions. 'Where are all the books?' he asks himself, out loud, somewhat implausibly. The next day he asks his mother, 'What have you done with Pa's first editions?' She says she had to sell a few things. 'Besides, those books were gathering dust,' she adds. Robert replies, 'Pa spent years building that collection. They weren't really yours to sell.' Well, they probably were, but it sounds like Robert had had his eye on them.

These first editions are absent, merely notional. Others are right there before our eyes. Like the jacketed US Doubleday hardback of Leon Uris's *Exodus* that lands heavily on Dalton Trumbo's desk a moment after Otto Preminger (Christian Berkel) has come to Trumbo's home on Christmas Day to persuade him to fix the script for the *Exodus* adaptation, in Jay

Roach's 2015 biopic of the blacklisted screenwriter, *Trumbo*, the title role played by Bryan Cranston. Or the Ballantine hardback of Ray Bradbury's *Fahrenheit 451* that Emily Watson parcels up to send to Bill Nighy along with paperbacks of Kingsley Amis's *That Uncertain Feeling* and Philip Larkin's *Collected Poems* in Isabel Coixet's *The Bookshop* (2017), an adaptation of Penelope Fitzgerald's novel. The novel is set in Suffolk, the film in Norfolk, but it is filmed, mostly, in Northern Ireland. The coastline is all wrong, but the books look right.

I preferred Isabel Coixet's contribution to the portmanteau film *Paris, je t'aime* (2006). In Coixet's segment, set in Bastille, a Lothario about to leave his wife for an air hostess changes his mind when his wife announces she's got terminal leukaemia. He eschews the cabin crew and treats his wife the way she's always wanted to be treated, which appears to include taking her to matinées of Béla Tarr films – well, they might start in the afternoon, but *Satantango* will be going on until late in the evening – and reading to her from Haruki Murakami's *Sputnik Sweetheart*.

The Coen Bros' contribution to the same film features a guide book, which hapless tourist Steve Buscemi is looking at while waiting for his train in the Tuileries metro station. Never make eye contact, the book tells him. Too late. He's eyeballing the woman on the opposite platform – the woman with the jealous boyfriend, who starts up with, 'Qu'est-ce que tu regardes, connard?', which Buscemi's book tells him means, 'What are you looking at, cunt (person)?' A short time later, bruised and lying on the platform, Buscemi feels the full weight of the contents of his bag as they are dropped on top of him, notably a very heavy-looking book called *Le Louvre*.

Béla Tarr was executive producer on *Lamb* (2021), directed by Valdimar Jóhannsson, which I watched on Mubi the night it was released on the streaming service. Normally I watch films on DVD, which seems to me to be a perfect technology. Blu-rays are fine, although I wish the boxes were the same size as those for DVDs. I don't mind being out of step with current trends. It means there are lots of DVDs in charity shops, because nobody want them apart from a few old gits clinging on to the past. Also, I can stop, go back, pause and so on, which I need to do a fair bit to identify some of these books. I know you can do that on streaming services, but it's often a bit fiddly, and DVDs look nice on shelves. A bit like books.

In *Lamb*, a folk horror film featuring a human/sheep hybrid, Maria is reading a book at the kitchen table. We can't see enough to identify it, but later, we see her reading the same book in bed. It's an Icelandic translation of a Mikhail Bulgakov novella called *Heart of a Dog*. In chapter three (the film is divided into three 'chapters', maybe Tarr's influence), Ingvar reads a bedtime story to Ada. It's 'The Story of Dimmalimm' by Godmundur Thorsteinsson. I recently found a copy of the Picador Classics edition of *Heart of a Dog*, but haven't read it yet. I didn't get on with Bulgakov's *The Master and Margarita*, the one time I tried to read it; I sense that *Heart of a Dog* might be a better bet for someone increasingly allergic to long novels.

I'm quite keen on folk horror, though, and was very excited to see Ben Wheatley's *In the Earth* (2021). Scientist Martin (Joel Fry) heads out on a two-day trek through the forest to meet up with old flame Dr Olivia Wendle (Hayley Squires). He is accompanied by park scout Alma (Ellora Torchia). On day two they come across an abandoned camp. The scout picks up and leafs through a pamphlet or children's book about the witch of local legend. Alma says she saw a camp like this before. Families come out, go sick . . .

Later, it all gets very silly, with Reece Shearsmith as Zach, the crazy guy in the woods, who captures Martin and Alma and feeds them drugged potion, eventually cutting off a couple of Martin's toes with an axe. Despite this they manage to escape and are rescued by Olivia, who at first seems legit, despite the revelation that Zach is her ex-hubby. Alma asks Olivia about her research and she launches into a breakneck speech about a stone that led her to a book that she runs to fetch from another tent. It contains, among other things, a convenient English translation of *Malleus Maleficarum*. The book is dated 1640 but some of its pages come from other, much older books. 'We're at the forefront of human discovery,' says Olivia, struggling to keep a straight face.

Just as *In the Earth* is not Ben Wheatley's best film, the ancient book reminds us of *The Ninth Gate* (1999), not only not Roman Polanski's best film, but so awful we've tried hard to forget it. Dean Corso (Johnny Depp) buys the four volumes of a 1780 edition of *Don Quixote* and takes them to his favourite rare bookdealer, Bernie, of Bernie's Rare Books. Corso heads off to a lecture being given by Boris Balkan PhD on Demons and Medieval Literature in the offices of Balkan Press. Boris takes him up to his private library and shows him his most prized volume, *The Nine Gates of the Kingdom of Shadows*, printed in Venice in 1666, the author and printer later being burned by the Holy Inquisition. Boris says he bought it off the old guy we saw hanging himself in the opening scene. Only three copies survive, says Corso. Only one, says Boris, who asks Corso if he's ever heard of a book written by Satan. At this point, we're losing the will to live, being no more into this than Johnny Depp appears to be. Balkan sends him off to Europe to compare the book with the other two surviving copies. At home, Corso sticks his dinner in the microwave as he looks at the book, which he later asks Bernie to look after for him. Poor Bernie – he's killed for the book, although the killers don't get the book. Instead of reporting the death, Corso flies to Spain to meet rare bookdealer twins, cartoon characters out of a bad children's film. Corso leaves and narrowly misses being killed by falling scaffolding, perhaps meant to represent the plot of the film. He goes to Portugal to visit Vargas, the owner of the other copy. Who should be in Corso's hotel than a woman from the Balkan lecture? She's in the lobby reading Dale Carnegie's *How to Win Friends and Influence People*. Together they go to see Vargas. They see him, but he doesn't see them, as he's dead in his goldfish pond, his copy of *The Nine Gates* burned to cinders in his grate. And so to Paris, where Corso visits Baroness Kessler, basically Mollie Sugden in a wheelchair. How could the director of *Rosemary's Baby* have put this mess together? It soon degenerates into a long and boring game of Spot the Difference (between engravings). Corso is about to speak when Mrs Slocombe tells him not to. In the Baroness's copy of the book, Corso finds an inclusion, a postcard from Boris to the Baroness: 'Sorry Frieda, I saw it first! Boris.' It's addressed to 17 quai d'Anjou, 75004 Paris, a real address on the Ile St Louis.

How to Win Friends and Influence People pops up again in Niels Mueller's *The Assassination of Richard Nixon* (2004). Sean Penn has dinner with his sales company boss who puts two books on the table: the Dale Carnegie and *The Power of Positive Thinking* by Norman Vincent Peale. 'These will make you a salesman,' he says. 'I guarantee it.'

We see *The Power of Positive Thinking* again in Guillermo del

Toro's *The Shape of Water* (2017); the evil boss man is reading it in his office. For me, this was the most interesting moment in the film, in fact the only interesting moment in the film. But let's think positively – about Polanski. If we look back at his earlier films, perhaps *The Ninth Gate* can be seen as an aberration. He loves his books, that's for sure. In Polanski's first feature, *Knife in the Water* (1962), the young hitch-hiker who gets in the couple's car does so with an original Polish edition of *What Every Driver Should Know!* by Henryk Galecki and Zygmunt Slabecki in his bag. The cover is almost impossible to see, but keen-eyed Twitter user Franz Propp identified it for me. Catherine Deveuve, meanwhile, cleaning human blood off the door of her sister's London flat in *Repulsion* (1965), does so with a copy of Betty MacDonald's *Anybody Can Do Anything* (Penguin).

Polanski directs himself as Trelkovsky, the title character, in *The Tenant* (1976). Trelkovsky looks through former tenant Simone Choule's belongings and finds nail varnish, a bra and a book – *Egypte*. At this point he has already found her tooth in a hole in the wall. Later, a man knocks on the door of the apartment. The man had been in love with Simone and had never told her. Trelkovsky takes him for a drink in a café where the man tells Trelkovsky he had sent Simone a postcard from the Egyptian department of the Louvre. Later still, at a gathering, an old friend of Simone's gives Trelkovsky a copy of one of Simone's books, *The Novel of the Mummy* by Théophile Gautier, a French edition from 1964. 'I haven't read it,' says Trelkovsky. 'Nor have I,' says the friend. (Me neither.) 'I'm not interested in Egyptology,' the friend continues. 'She left it behind one evening. You can have it if you like.' Trelkovsky replies, 'Oh, you're very kind. I would love to read it.' In a later scene, Trelkovsky sits in the apartment applying Simone's red nail varnish. The bottle stands on his table next to another book whose cover image suggests an Ancient Egyptian theme, whether a novel or non-fiction is unclear, as we don't see enough to identify it. Maybe the Gautier prop went missing and this was a stand-in?

Saturday 17 July 2010

Talking to someone in New York who had some kind of list and on it – the top two items – were my books *The Matter of the Heart* and *The Director's Cut*. Not the novels, though: film adaptations, but in some hard-to-define way, not proper films.

What motivates an author or film-maker to make a new work and give it the same title as an existing work? In *The Tenant* (2012), directed by Chris Jaymes, David Arquette plays a writer who moves into a cottage (indeed, the film is known as *The Cottage* in the US) in the garden of a composer-teacher and his family. When his prospective future landlords ask him what he does, he says he writes 'romance novels'. He's written 'fourteen so far', he says, and his demographic loves them. 'What are the names of some of your novels?' asks the composer's wife, like novels have names. 'The one I just finished was *Nicole's in Love* and before that *Kate's Dream* and before that *Megan's Games*,' he says, reeling off these titles of novels that are imaginary even within the hopelessly unbelievable world of the film. This bloke, we soon find out, or intuit, has never written a word in his life, although Nicole, Kate and Megan all exist, back in his mountain hideaway. They're his implausibly smitten and soon-to-be mur-derous harem. In the acknowledgements at the end of the film, if we stick around that long, we find an interesting name – Jack Nicholson – who, in Jack Torrance, played someone else who claimed to be writing books and wasn't, but at least Jack did some typing, which is half way there.

In Stanley Kubrick's *The Shining* (1980), while Jack is having his job interview, at the Overlook Hotel, his wife Wendy (Shelley Duval) is at home in their kitchen looking after their son, Danny (Danny Lloyd). Danny is eating a sandwich and Wendy is reading *The Catcher in the Rye*. JD Salinger's novel is one of a large number of books that are burned in François Truffaut's *Fahrenheit 451* (1966), an adaptation of the Ray Bradbury novel that, as noted earlier, Emily Watson sends to Bill Nighy in *The Bookshop* (2017). In *Fahrenheit 451*, firemen start fires rather than put them out. On his suspended monorail train home from work, fireman Montag (Oskar Werner) meets Clarisse, a schoolteacher, played by Julie Christie. They get off at the same stop and she asks him, 'Tell me, why do you burn books?' He says, 'It's a job like any other. Good work, lots of variety. Monday we burn Miller, Tuesday Tolstoy, Wednesday Walt Whitman, Friday Faulkner and Saturday and Sunday Schopenhauer and Sartre. We burn them to ashes and then burn the ashes. It's our official motto.' He goes on, 'Books are just so much rubbish. They have no interest.'

She asks, 'Then why do some people still read them, although it's so dangerous?'

'Precisely because it is forbidden,' he answers.

'Why is it forbidden?' she asks.

'Because it makes people unhappy,' he tells her.

'Do you really believe that?'

'Oh yes. Books disturb people. They make them anti-social.'

Joining *The Catcher in the Rye* in the pitiless flames, among many other famous and less-celebrated titles, is Raymond Chandler's *The Big Sleep*. In Howard Hawks's 1946 adaptation of Chandler's novel, Philip Marlowe (Humphrey Bogart) is summoned to see Vivian Rutledge (Lauren Bacall), who says, 'So you're a private detective. I didn't know they existed except in books.'

In regard to the job Marlowe is taking on for her father, General Sternwood, she asks, 'What will your first step be?' He answers, 'The usual one.' She says, 'I didn't know there was a usual one.' 'Sure there is,' he says. 'It comes complete with diagrams on page forty-seven of *How to be a Detective in Ten Easy Lessons*, correspondence school textbook.'

The next scene finds him at Hollywood Public Library looking at chapter 14 of *Famous First Editions*, a chapter headed 'Collectors' Items'. Marlowe makes a note – 'Chevalier Audubon' – before visiting a second-hand bookshop, AG Geiger Rare Books, Geiger's name having been at the bottom of a note Sternwood had shown him. Mindful of what the librarian had told him – that he didn't look like the kind of man who would be interested in first editions – before he enters the shop he turns up the brim of his fedora and puts on a pair of dark glasses. Adopting a manner it might be anachronistic to call geeky or nerdy, he asks the sultry but suspicious-looking woman in the shop, 'Would you happen to have a *Ben Hur*, 1860?'

'A first edition?' she asks. 'No, no, no,' he says, 'the third, the one with the erratum slip on page 116 . . . How about a Chevalier 1840, full set, of course?' 'Not at the moment.' 'You do sell books, hmm?' he says, looking over his glasses. 'What do those look like? Grapefruit?' she says. 'From here they look like books. Maybe I'd better see Mr Geiger?'

But Mr Geiger is not available to the likes of Marlowe, so he goes across the road to Acme Book Shop, where he asks the girl with glasses – so, obviously a real bookseller, unlike the femme fatale across the street – for the same books. She says they don't exist. As he hangs around the shop to watch for Geiger, she removes her glasses, at his prompting, and lets her hair down.

Later, Vivian Rutledge goes to see Marlowe in his office. 'So you do get up,' she says. 'I was beginning to think you worked in bed like Marcel Proust.'

'Who's he?' asks Marlowe.

'You wouldn't know him. French writer.'

'Come into my boudoir.'

I could watch this stuff all day.

As could director Mike Hodges, who was also a fan of Chandler. Three minutes into Hodges' directorial debut, 1971 British gangster movie *Get Carter*, Jack Carter (Michael Caine) is on a train to Newcastle sitting in first class and reading Chandler's *Farewell, My Lovely*. He's not far in and he's no further in several hours later as night falls and he arrives in Newcastle. We've enjoyed shots during the journey of the sun in the sky due north of the train, a mystery in itself, and a Deltic hoovering past in the opposite direction, a more convincing detail. The cover of *Farewell, My Lovely* is not one that can be found online, weirdly, and yet why would the production designer bother creating a mock-up of a fictitious edition? What would have been the point? We don't see any more books until ten minutes from the end when John Osborne calls his driver into his book-lined study to set him up, poor bastard, as a sacrificial lamb.

The following year found Caine in a theatrical two-hander with Laurence Olivier. *Sleuth* (1972) was directed by Joseph Mankiewicz and written by Anthony Shaffer, adapting his own play. Olivier plays bestselling author Andrew Wyke, Caine a hairdresser called Milo Tindle who is having an affair with the older man's wife. The two meet in Wyke's country house, where

Wyke pulls one of his own books from the shelf. 'Surely you've read it?' he says. Tindle shakes his head. 'Pity,' says the author, 'an absolute corker.' The film has its fans, who might describe it in the same terms, among them French author Tanguy Viel, whose 1999 novel *Cinéma*, is literally all about it, and Kenneth Branagh, who remade the film in 2008 with Caine in the Olivier role and Jude Law playing the part previously played by Caine (as he had also done in the 2004 remake of *Alfie*). When Caine invites Law into his 'special book room', I think of Irish novelist John Boyne ushering interviewers into his 'ego room'.

'These are all my novels. You've read them, I suppose?' says Caine. 'Afraid not,' says Law. On the wall we see a poster produced by his supposed publishers, Baron Books. 'The master of menace,' says the *Sunday Times*. Titles are listed: *Rat in a Trap*, *Blackout*, *The Obelisk*, *The Cats Whiskers* (no apostrophe), *Blind Mans Buff* (ditto), *Losers Kiss* (ditto). The heart sinks, but Branagh's *Sleuth* is at least an improvement on George Mihalka's *Bullet to Beijing* (1995), which sought to resurrect the career of the unnamed agent in Len Deighton's novels *The Ipcress File*, *Funeral in Berlin* and *Billion Dollar Brain*, named as Harry Palmer and played by Caine, in the films directed by, respectively, Sidney J Furie, Guy Hamilton and Ken Russell.

In *Bullet to Beijing*, Palmer is summoned to see his boss, who introduces him to the idea of accelerated retirement. A blow, but one softened by an immediate offer of freelance work from shadowy employers who send Palmer an air ticket. 'St Petersburg,' Palmer says to himself, adding, 'Russia.' In Russia, after a car chase and, for good measure – it is St Petersburg, after all – a boat chase, Palmer meets his employer, Michael Gambon, who offers him $250,000 ('That's £180,000,' Palmer muses) to retrieve a biological weapon before it finds its way to

North Korea. Gambon's accent suggests he's enjoying himself – when we can hear it over Rick Wakeman's insistent, soaring score – but there are no signs that Michael Caine feels anything apart from shame. Following another chase – on foot this time – Palmer leaves his hotel by the window and settles down on the night train to Beijing with a hardback edition of O Henry. O Harry, more like, whatever possessed you? Ah yes, the £180,000 – and the rest.

What have films and hotel bedside drawers got in common? Often, a copy of the Bible. In Christopher Nolan's *Memento* (2000) there's a Gideon's Bible in the bedside drawer of the motel room where Leonard Shelby (Guy Pearce) wakes up. Much later, or earlier (Leonard has anterograde amnesia and the film keeps going backwards), he's putting a book on the fire. It doesn't have a cover. Then we see Natalie (Carrie-Anne Moss) reading it in bed. He says to her, 'How can you read that again?' She says, 'It's good.' 'Yeah, but you've read it like a thousand times.' 'I enjoy it.' 'I always thought the pleasure of a book was in wanting to know what happens next.' 'Don't be a prick. I'm not reading it to annoy you. I enjoy it. Just let me read, please.' Yeah, just let her read. What's she reading? It took some effort, but it turns out to be Robert Graves' *Claudius the God*.

In prison in Stanley Kubrick's *A Clockwork Orange* (1970) Alex DeLarge (Malcolm McDowell) becomes very interested in the 'Big Book'.

Do e-Bibles count? In the otherwise largely uninteresting *Alien Resurrection* (1997), directed by Jean-Pierre Jeunet, Ripley (Sigourney Weaver) picks up an electronic copy of the Holy Bible. 'Old and New Testaments. Newly Edited by the Revision Committee.' There's a date that is, sadly, unreadable, and then it says, 'Press to start.' Instead, Ripley unplugs it.

Less believable, but more fun, is Andrzej Zulawski's totally bonkers *Possession* (1981). Sam Neill is the least plausible spy in the history of spy films, but we only see him at work near the beginning, where he attends an unconvincing meeting, and towards the end, where he's involved in a shootout with a man wearing pink socks. The real story has to do with the relationship between Isabelle Adjani and Neill, who both seem to be one giggle away from corpsing throughout the entire film, as Neill widens his eyes so far you worry they might fall out and Adjani twists and turns in fits and spasms. But then she is possessed. There's some kind of creature growing in a darkened room that shows more genuine emotion than either of the stars. Early on, Neill is searching in their apartment for clues as to where 'downtown' – funny term to use in the context of West Berlin – Adjani might have gone. Naturally this requires him to run his fingers along the spines of the books on their bookshelf: *Ontologie* by Georg Lukacs; *Principles of Perception* by S Howard Bartley; *Touching: Significance of the Skin* by Ashley Montagu; a German translation of *Cults of Unreason* by Christopher Evans; and, of course, The Holy Bible.

The street preacher in John Carpenter's *They Live* (1988) has a red bible. At a magazine stand where all the magazines order readers, if they're wearing the magic shades, to STAY ASLEEP and OBEY, there are also books, including *Wifey* by Judy Blume. With the glasses on, it has a white cover bearing only the words NO THOUGHT.

Saturday 7 October 2017
Passing through Macclesfield with my girlfriend. We were in the town centre, although it looked different. I saw a second-hand bookshop I'd never seen before. It had some connection with

Poynton. I couldn't go there now, however, because, although it didn't look like it, we were on the train and couldn't get off. I told myself I'd go another time.

Writers, whether starting out or established, are hard to get right. Keith Allen is unconvincing as Hugo in Danny Boyle's *Shallow Grave* (1994), but there's a good reason for that and it has to do with the suitcase full of money under his bed. Neither Max (Vincent Cassel) in Gilles Mimouni's *The Apartment* (1996) nor Paul (Alec Newman) in Penny Woolcock's *The Principles of Lust* (2003) has that excuse.

Jack Manfred (Clive Owen) is writing a novel, *The Ball*, in Mike Hodges' *Croupier* (1998). After a meeting with his publisher friend Giles, who plays a fruit machine in his office, in which Giles says, 'Let me give you three words of advice. Don't give up,' Jack comes up with three words for Giles: 'Go fuck yourself.' But, at home, working on *The Ball*, he changes the title to *On the Ball*. On the tube, after getting a job at the casino and selling his car to get cash before his pay comes through, he is surrounded by people reading books. Those were the days. We see Donald Zec and Anthony Fowles's biography of Barbra Streisand. 'Jack imagined people reading his book,' goes the interior monologue. 'One day he would get into their heads. Play with their imagination. Test their feelings.' Another passenger is reading a book on assertiveness, *When I Say No, I Feel Guilty*, by Manuel J Smith.

Jack tells his girlfriend Marion (Gina McKee) he's sold his car. She says he should take the money back and sell his book. She's betting on him, she says. Later, he quotes Hemingway to the colleague who takes him to a gambling den. He rewrites his novel and Marion reads it. There's no hope, she complains. It's the truth, he insists. In Waterstone's he buys a copy of John

Scarne's *Scarne on Card Tricks* and spots Giles, whose author Habib is launching his terrorist memoir *Death Squad*. It's a 'kill and tell book', says Giles. 'Books piled like chips,' Jack tells us. 'Stack 'em high, sell 'em fast, make a killing. No dumb soccer novel for Jack. He would write about the world he knew, from the inside . . . Here was an interesting question. Was writing work or play?' Later, Jack sees his book in a window display. *I Croupier* by Anonymous.

One of the girls Juliette Binoche interviews for her article on students working as sex workers in Malgoska Szumowska's *Elles* (2011) goes to see a man about a room in an apartment. The man says he wants her to dust around his books before asking her if he can see her breasts. There you have it in a nutshell, what makes French cinema irresistible to a certain kind of man: sex and books.

Danish director Jens Jorgen Thorsen's *Quiet Days in Clichy* (1970) isn't actually French, but is pretending to be. A writer, Joey, and his friend, Carl, share an apartment and a number of women. One woman asks Joey for money for sex and he re-members that Carl has 200 francs hidden in his copy of Goethe's *Faust*. He takes the book from the shelf and removes the cash and pays for the sex. There's a lot of sex in this film. It's basically a sex film with some innovative touches like thought bubbles and writing on the screen. The most interesting parts are where Joey walks through the streets of Paris. Later, Joey is picking up a girl in a café. She looks at a book he has on the table in front of him. We can't see what book it is. She says, 'I don't read so many books. It's too much for my feeble brain. There are lots of other things to do in life.' Cut to them getting undressed.

Certified Copy (2010), directed by Abbas Kiarostami, is a French-Italian co-production, but could not be any more French.

There's a book in shot right from the start. It's called *Certified Copy* and is a non-fiction book about copies and originals in art by James Miller. It's not the English novelist James Miller, author of *Lost Boys* and *Sunshine State*, but a fictitious author played by William Shimell who arrives to address a room full of Italian fans. He's horribly pompous but generously does not get irritated by Juliette Binoche's antiques dealer in the front row dealing with her bored son and, indeed, getting up to leave with him. Then Miller's phone rings and two unbelievable things happen. Firstly, he answers it and, secondly, Binoche finds this funny and charming. Later, she takes him for a drive. They go in a museum, then in a café where they have a coffee. She steps outside to take a phone call. He joins her and they leave without paying, but no one pursues them. Later still, Miller and Binoche go in a restaurant and he clicks his fingers at the waiter, like he's Mr Big, and I suddenly realise who he's been reminding me of all through the film, Big in *Sex and the City*. After a row, they leave without paying for their wine and no one pursues them from the restaurant either.

The sex in French films, of course, often involves mistresses. In Claude Chabrol's *The Girl Cut in Two* (2007), Gabrielle is a weather forecaster in Lyon who lives with her mother. She gets into a relationship with married bestselling author Charles Saint Denis, whose editor arrives at his beautiful modern home in the countryside with a boot full of copies of his latest book, *L'absence de Pénélope*. He's got to sign books for a local bookseller who is afraid he'll run out of stock. 'We're printing two to three hundred thousand,' his editor says. 'You can't complain.' He says, 'I'm not complaining.'

Saint Denis takes Gabrielle to an auction where he bids for and wins a rare edition of *La femme et le pantin* by Pierre Louÿs in perfect condition from 1937. Bidding opens at 500 euro and closes at 2000. Charles gives the book to Gabrielle and they go back to his apartment. While he's opening the celebratory champagne she takes a book from the shelf, *Manuel de Civilité pour les petites filles à l'usage des maisons d'education* – another one by Louÿs. Later, Saint Denis tells Gabrielle he's got to go to London tomorrow. They had to bring it forward, he tells her, because Jonathan Coe had a clash.

'It was a weird feeling being mentioned in that film,' Jonathan Coe tells me, 'especially by such an unpleasant character. Kind of flattering too, though, I suppose, to be a point of reference.'

Henry James pops up in at least two French films. In *Confidences trop intimes* (2004) directed by Patrice Leconte, Anna (Sandrine Bonnaire) picks up a book in the office of M Faber (Fabrice Luchini), *La bête dans le jungle*. 'Is it set in Africa with wild animals?' she asks. 'No,' Faber replies, 'it's set in England with people who are a little grey, melancholic. I'll lend it you if you want.' She thanks him and puts it in her bag. (I look the book up. It's *The Beast in the Jungle* by Henry James.) Later, she returns it. 'It's not for me,' she says. In Agnès Jaoui's *Le goût des autres* (2000), a boorish businessman falls for his English teacher, but she finds his old-fashioned values and behaviour offensive. Also, she doesn't like moustaches, so he shaves his off. But it's going to take more than that. In an English tea room he gives her back two borrowed books. One is Henry James's *Portrait of a Lady*, of which he's read only four pages. We don't see what the other one is.

Some French films are not French at all, but British, like *Le Week-end* (2013), directed by Roger Michell and written by Hanif Kureishi. Married couple Meg (Lindsay Duncan) and Nick (Jim Broadbent) return to Paris, the scene of their honeymoon, but bicker rather than reminisce. Luckily, Morgan (Jeff Goldblum), an old friend of Nick's, is around to cheer us all up. A *New York Times*-bestselling author, he signs a copy of his novel for Nick. When I see the title page, my mood darkens again. The title appears as 'Read my Lips', whereas I feel sure most publishers would prefer 'Read My Lips', or, as it's French, despite the title being in English, 'Read my lips'. Below that we read, 'Traduit de l'américain par Paul Jonhson.' The first time I saw 'Traduit de l'américain' in a French book, I thought it was a mistake, but it's not. That's what they say if the author is American rather than British. 'Jonhson', however, surely is a mistake.

I put on Jim Jarmusch's *Mystery Train* (1989) after his *Night on Earth* (1991) and was just starting to wonder if there's any point to watching a Jim Jarmusch film when we moved into the second story in *Mystery Train*, in which a heartbroken widow signs multiple forms at an airport for the passage home to Italy of her husband's coffin, and my interest was finally engaged. She goes to make a phone call and suddenly seems less heartbroken. She finishes the call clutching a brick of a book – Ludovico Ariosto's *Orlando Furioso*, a sixteenth-century epic poem, apparently, although you probably knew that. She's got a red bookmark in near the beginning of the book. When she gets out of a taxi moments later the bookmark is nearer the middle of the book. I mean, I don't blame her for skimming and dipping in and out when it comes to epic verse. Then, after buying a load of magazines, she is in a diner reading the book when Tom Noonan sits down opposite her and tells her a story about Elvis. When Noonan bothers her again outside the diner, her bookmark has returned to nearer the beginning of the book. Later, when she's in bed trying to read and the roommate from New Jersey won't shut up, she's right in the middle of the book.

A lot of people read in bed. I used to, but nowadays it just makes me fall asleep. I can read out loud to my wife, when she has asked me to do so. Indeed, I have been reading her sections of this book while writing it. I started reading her this chapter one night and got two pages in before she stopped reacting. The next time we tried it, I didn't quite reach the end of the first paragraph before her breathing slowed.

In Kore-eda Hirokazu's *The Truth* (2019), grand actress Fabienne (Catherine Deneuve) is giving an interview at home to a somewhat bewitched male journalist to mark the publication of her memoir when her daughter Lumir (Juliette Binoche) and son-in-law Hank (Ethan Hawke) and granddaughter turn up from New York. Interestingly, they approach via the back garden, across the lawn on which no desire path has been worn, despite the fact that all family members come and go this way (only unexpected visitors come to the front door). Lumir is angry that her mother has published the book – *La Vérité* – without letting her vet any content relating to her. There's an extended shot where they stand alongside each other, each holding a copy of the book and turning it around in their hands. Later, Lumir, in bed, reads the book and makes notes on it.

In the brilliant *Lemming* (2005), directed by Dominik Moll, immediately following the early, excruciating scene in which Richard (André Dussollier) and his wife Alice (Charlotte Rampling) arrive late for dinner at the home of Alain (Laurent Lucas) and Bénédicte (Charlotte Gainsbourg) and have a terrible row, Laurent is seen reading in bed next to the sleeping Bénédicte. It took me a long time to work out what he's reading. Silverberg and Strindberg were both in the frame before I finally identified the author – in fact, the editor – as Bruce Sterling. It's the French edition of his landmark cyberpunk short story anthology *Mirror-*

shades. In a later scene, after Alice has visited Alain at work and kissed him, Alain returns home and Bénédicte is reading on the sofa. You smell weird, she tells him. You smell of soap. Sadly she has the front cover of her book folded over the back.

In Nicolas Bedos's *La belle époque* (2019) – *excusez-moi* for all the French films, but they put more books in their films than we do or the Americans do – Daniel Auteuil and Fanny Ardant are in bed. She's got a VR headset on and he is reading Patrick Modiano's *In the Café of Lost Youth* (in the original French edition from Gallimard. I read my Folio edition in the autumn of 2023, the perfect time of year to read it. 'For me,' writes the narrator, in my own clumsy translation, 'autumn has never been a season of sadness. Dead leaves and shorter days have never evoked, for me, the end of something, but rather anticipation of things to come. On October evenings, as night falls, there's electricity in the air in Paris'). Auteuil says he likes simply having to turn the page to find out what happens next. Then he chucks the book on the floor and he and Ardant have an argument. He says, 'Nobody buys books.' She counters: 'Nobody buys your books.'

There's a poignancy in Modiano's *In the Café of Lost Youth*, as there is in most of his books, to do with the past, with the fact that it *is* the past and unrecoverable, but I wonder how much of that poignancy is the reader's projecting on to it. Modiano's characters are not mired in sadness as they dwell on the past. *In the Café of Lost Youth* is, nevertheless, a good choice for Auteil, a disillusioned illustrator sceptical of a new form of time-travel entertainment. Similarly carefully chosen props find their way into the hands of Jonathan and Alice in Christophe Honoré's *Dans Paris* (2006). Ex-lovers, Jonathan and Alice argue about money, fool around and end up in bed, where she lights a post-coital cigarette and he reads a French edition of JD Salinger's *Franny and Zooey*. They start arguing again and he picks up another book, Alice Munro's *The Love of a Good Woman*, again in French translation.

May I try the reader's patience with just one more book at bedtime before moving on? It is to be found in Anthony Mann's *A Dandy in Aspic* (1968), an adaptation of Derek Marlowe's spy novel. Alexander Eberlin (Laurence Harvey) wants to go back to Moscow after eighteen years as a double agent in London. He makes a request and is told the answer will come in the morning, at the church. At the church, in the morning, Eberlin reaches into the shadows for a hymn book with a red ribbon. Inside he finds a piece of paper on which is written, simply, 'NO'.

Later, Eberlin, as George Dancer, enters the hotel room of his lover, Caroline (Mia Farrow), and finds her asleep in bed, a splayed green-spined Penguin paperback on the bed beside her. The book is a spy novel, *Eyes For Spies* by Nick Mann, actually rather poorly mocked up, with a Penguin logo on the front cover that's too big and type on the spine and back cover that looks slightly off, too. But it's the thought that counts. Nick Mann was the director's son and could only have been three or four years old at the time; Nick's mother was Anthony Mann's third wife, ballerina Anna Kuzko.

Anthony Mann died during the shooting of the film in West Berlin. He suffered a heart attack in his hotel room on 29 April 1967. Direction was finished off by Laurence Harvey.

Wednesday 7 February 2018
John Foxx told me he wanted to read my novel set on the Isle of Skye. I can't remember if I'd written one or not.

What's your favourite film? Are there any books in it? While

I'm waiting, I'll tell you that my favourite film is Nicolas Roeg's *Don't Look Now* (1973).

Since I started looking for books in films, it has changed the way I watch films. I watch now with pen and notebook to hand, like when I went to press shows as a novice reviewer for my school newspaper and then my college newspaper. For a brief spell, from 2008 to 2010, I fulfilled an ambition to be the film reviewer for a more widely circulated publication when the *London Magazine*, under the editorship of Sara-Mae Tuson, indulged me. It was a privilege to at least try on the shoes of Roy Armes, who had been the magazine's film critic in the 1970s. His 1976 book *The Ambiguous Image* (Secker & Warburg) had a strong influence on the development of my taste. I grew to love European arthouse cinema as much as the horror films I had been drawn to more instinctively.

Don't Look Now swims in both these streams – or should I say canals? John Baxter (Donald Sutherland) is inspecting a series of slides of a church interior and spots a red-hooded figure sitting in a pew. He speaks the first line of dialogue, to his wife Laura (Julie Christie): 'What are you reading?'

She says, 'I was just trying to find the answer to a question Christine was asking me. If the world is round, why is a frozen pond flat?' She puts the book down on the settee – at this point we can't see what it is – and picks up another.

As John leans to take the slide out of the projector, he reaches across a book on his desk, *The Art of Illumination* (by P D'Ancona and E Aeschlimann, published by Phaidon), and says it's a good question. He uses a magnifying glass and a light box to have a closer look at the red-hooded figure.

Laura finds that Lake Ontario curves more than three degrees from its easternmost shore to its westernmost shore. 'So,' she says, 'frozen water isn't flat.' John adds: 'Nothing is what it seems.' Possibly the most important line in the film.

John has his premonition and leaves the room, dropping the slide on the settee where Laura is sitting. She picks it up and looks at it and drops it on the cover of the first book she had been looking at, which we now see bears the title *Beyond the Fragile Geometry of Space*. We can just read the name of the author: John Baxter. Can we assume it's the same John Baxter who only a moment ago spoke the line, 'Nothing is what it seems'? If it's John's book, why, when John asked her what she was reading, didn't Laura say she was reading his book, or looking in his book for the answer to the question Christine had asked? Why instead does she immediately put his book aside and pick up another book, a thicker book, more of an encyclopaedia-type book, the book in which she finds the answer to the question?

I must have seen *Don't Look Now* a dozen times – fifteen, maybe twenty – and yet only after I started looking for books in films did I spot this. (People, including artist and designer John Coulthart, spotted it before I did, I see.) And only when I watch it a thirteenth time – or a sixteenth, or twenty-first – do I see something else. It's long been the case that I find the film as powerfully moving as I find it frightening. Obviously, having seen a film this many times, you know what's coming next. You know what happens in the end. Just as we all know what happens at the end – of life. No matter how much you may wish you could change the outcome – whether we're talking about the film or about life – you can't. Maybe that partly explains why, every time I watch it, I feel it more deeply. What happens is avoidable; there are lots of warnings. Red for danger. The moment when John sees Laura and the two sisters at the prow of a boat that passes him on the Grand Canal, when Laura is supposed to be in, or on her way to, England, still frightens me every time I see it, but over time, with repeated viewings, I have started to find it, as I say, as sad as it is scary. Maybe because of how it links to the end of the film and exactly *how* it links is interesting, because the details are different, suggesting that even at that point, on the Grand Canal, there was some wiggle room. John could still have paid more attention to the nature of the warning. However, even as he gazed after the departing boat, he was looking in the wrong direction. Going to the police, who couldn't be less interested. Running around looking for Laura. He was wasting his time. Just as I know I'm wasting my time when I give in to anxieties about health. *Hi, my name is Axillary Lump. I'll be your possible symptom of lymphoma.*

Did I put *Don't Look Now* on a pedestal because it speaks to my anxiety or is it connected to my anxiety because of how much I love it? Did it contribute to the formation of my anxiety and have I unwittingly encouraged that to grow over the years by forever rewatching this bloody film?

For a lot of people, *the* talking point in *Don't Look Now* is the notorious love scene. Somehow a rumour got around that Donald Sutherland and Julie Christie were actually doing it. It doesn't seem to matter how many times the small number of people who were actually in the room deny that sex took place, the rumour persists. I'm much more interested in the fact that on the bedside table, throughout the love scene, there lies a book. The book, *Der Stell-Vertreter* by Rolf Hochhuth, published in Britain as *The Representative* and in the US as *The Deputy*, contains the script of a play by Hochhuth and a number of essays.

The anonymous author of the Freakydog blog muses on the possible reasons for the book's presence on that tightly controlled set. Is it to imply that not only can John get by in Italian, but he can also read German? Or could it have more to do with the play's subject matter, Pope Pius XII's failure to speak out against the Holocaust, and John's decision to take on a job for the Catholic church. As Freakyblog writes, 'Roeg only knows.'

Less puzzling is the presence of Jorge Luis Borges's *A Personal Anthology* in Roeg and Donald Cammell's *Performance* (1970). Rosie (Stanley Meadows) is reading a copy of the recently published 1969 Cape hardback edition in the back of the parked Rover, while Moody (John Bindon) occupies the driver's seat and Chas (James Fox) is visiting a small business to collect protection money. A short time later, the Borges is glimpsed on top of Harry Flowers' bed next to the *Jewish Chronicle*, Harry Flowers being the mob boss who runs the protection racket. How it ends up in Turner's (Mick Jagger's) hands at the Powis Square flat in Ladbroke Grove is anybody's guess. Turner reads from it, from the story 'The South', to Pherber (Anita Pallenberg) and the 'thin bird', Lucy (Michèle Breton). Turner reads four or five lines from an edited passage just a couple of paragraphs away from the end of the story. Then, irritated by a fly, he tosses the book on the floor.

A different book on a different floor, *The Soul of the Ape* by Eugène Marais is spotted in the hotel room of Locke (Jack Nicholson), somewhere in Saharan Africa, in Michelangelo Antonioni's *The Passenger* (1975). Also in Locke's room, on Locke's bed, is the body of Robertson, who died of natural causes in his own room, but Locke seizes the opportunity to switch. Not just rooms, but identities.

Later, in London, Locke walks down a set of steps in the Brunswick Centre and sees Maria Schneider, whose character is known simply as the girl, sitting on a bench reading. Actually, since Locke is now calling himself Robertson, it might be less confusing if I just call him Jack Nicholson and the girl Maria Schneider. She's not reading a book, however, so why have I mentioned it? Well, because when I first saw *The Passenger*, probably at the Scala in King's Cross, I lived just up the road in a university hall of residence, and one day we came down to the Brunswick Centre, my friends Alison, Julian and I, and we set up a photo in which Alison played Maria Schneider and Julian took Jack Nicholson's part. Alison sat on the bench reading and Julian came down the steps and I took a photo and sadly I don't know where that photo is, but it's probably somewhere, unlike the steps, which were removed a few years later.

Also, I'm incapable of seeing the words 'Brunswick Centre' without thinking of Skoob Books, which probably hasn't been mentioned in this book often enough yet.

Jack Nicholson and Maria Schneider get together later and share a hotel room. The Eugène Marais book, which we thought had been left in Jack's hotel room with the body of Robertson, purporting to be the body of Locke, don't forget, turns out to have come with them. However, when Locke's widow – I mean, she's not really his widow, as he's still alive, but she has been told he's dead, and anyway, I should have said Jack Nicholson's widow – gets his personal effects back, the Eugène Marais book is among them.

The film is a lot less confusing than my description of it. I included it at this point because the wandering copy of *The Soul of the Ape* by Eugène Marais reminds me of the ubiquitous copy of Borges's *A Personal Anthology* in *Performance*. Although, who's to say Rosie didn't give his copy to Harry Flowers, and Turner had his own copy all along?

My favourite living British film-maker, since Nicolas Roeg died, is Joanna Hogg. I rewatched her films – no hardship – to check for books, having a feeling I would not be wasting my time. If only Anna (Kathryn Worth) in *Unrelated* (2007) had taken a closer look at the cover of the book she opens on her first morning by the pool – Dante's *The Divine Comedy, 1. Hell* – she might have been better prepared for the holiday to come. In *Archipelago* (2010), at the start of a short break on Tresco with sister Cynthia (Lydia Leonard) and mother Patricia (Kate Fahy), Edward (Tom Hiddleston) spends a bit of time arranging his books on his bedside table, but we never see what they are. At the end of the film, as they are preparing to leave, Cynthia says to Patricia, 'I've got one of your books.' Patricia says, 'Oh have you?' Cynthia: 'I'll give it back to you.' Patricia: 'Which one?' Cynthia: 'The Boyd.' Patricia: 'Oh great. Did you enjoy it?' Cynthia: 'I barely started it.'

In both *Exhibition* (2013) and *The Souvenir* (2019), characters read out loud to their partners. In *Exhibition*, H (Liam Gillick) reads to D (Viv Albertine), in bed, from Hermann Hesse's *Steppenwolf*, and in *The Souvenir*, Julie (Honor Swinton Byrne) reads to Anthony (Tom Burke) from a book about Venice, *The City of Beautiful Nonsense* by Ernest Temple Thurston. Loose at the back of the book are some photographs of Anthony, including one taken in Afghanistan, he says. Anthony claims to work at the Foreign Office, but cultivates an air of secrecy and mystery, whether because he is legally required to or because it makes it easier to hide his heroin habit is left deliberately unclear. Later, Julie's flatmate is moving out so that Anthony can move in. 'Is this my book?' Julie says to the boy who's moving out, showing him a book we don't get a good look at. 'Yes,' he says. She tells him he can keep it. 'All right, cheers,' he says. In *The Souvenir Part II* (2021), when Julie visits Anthony's parents, Anthony's father says he is reading a Chapman Pincher book about people working for the Foreign Office leading double lives, but the book we can see lying on top of a bookcase behind him as he speaks, with a bookmark sticking out of it, is Andrew Boyle's *The Climate of Treason: Five Who Spied For Russia.*

There seem to be fewer books in Christopher Nolan's films as his career proceeds. In Nolan's low-budget black and white debut, *Following* (1998), still my favourite of his films, Cobb (Alex Haw) breaks into a flat with Bill (Jeremy Theobald) in tow. 'From the futon and the shared laundry bag,' Cobbs says, 'they must be over 25.' Bill says, 'They could be 20 and have been living together for years.' 'No,' says Cobb. 'Look at the books.' We look at the books – Jonathan Raban's *Old Glory*, *The Works of Oscar Wilde*, Ludovic Kennedy's *On My Way to the Club*, Daniel J Borstin's *The Discoverers*, AS Byatt's *Possession*, Peter Mayle's *Toujours Provence*, an Isabel Allende that might be *The Stories of Eva Luna*, Bruce Chatwin's *In Patagonia*, and then two more Picadors, one of which is probably Nabokov's *Lectures on Literature* and another that is either Julian Barnes's *A History of the World in 10½ Chapters* or Elias Canetti's *The Conscience of Words* and *Earwitness*. 'They're college-educated. Probably graduated when they were 21 or 22. Moved in together in the last year. You can tell more from the music.'

Some other favourite directors don't do books in films, or not many. Hitchcock – not many books. In *Vertigo* (1958), Midge (Barbara Bel Geddes) takes Johnny (James Stewart) to the Argosy Bookshop so he can ask the bookseller about Carlotta Valdes, but that's about it, apart from the catalogue Johnny obtains at the art gallery at the Palace of the Legion of Honour.

David Lynch – not many books. Indeed, a few minutes into *Lost Highway* (1997), Renée (Patricia Arquette) says to Fred

(Bill Pullman), 'You don't mind that I'm not coming to the club tonight?' He says, 'What are you gonna do?' She says, 'Stay home. Read.' He says, 'Read?' He repeats, 'Read? Read what?' He might well ask. There are no books in Fred and Renée's scary house, just a TV/VCR, a saxophone and lots of mother-in-law's tongues.

There's more reported reading without any evidence of actual books in Brian De Palma's *Carlito's Way* (1993). Lalin Miasso (Viggo Mortensen) tells Carlito (Al Pacino) how he got through his time in jail – reading – but the only books in sight in this overlong 1970s-set gangster movie are red leather-bound ones in the District Attorney's office. I watched *Carlito's Way* after discovering that it was the last film cartoonist and *Penguin Modern Stories* contributor Mel Calman ever saw, although he didn't see it in its entirety. Calman suffered a heart attack while watching the film at the Empire Leicester Square, in February 1994, in the company of his partner Deborah Moggach.

7

Three reminiscences

'Tonight or tomorrow, Royle?'

'Tonight, please, sir.'

'Half an hour or an hour?'

'Half an hour, please, sir.'

'Right, Royle, that's one hour tomorrow night.'

You could substitute Radcliffe – or Balinski, Greenwood, Henderson or Wilson – for Royle, and you could have the pupil ask for an hour, in the hope that Mr Farquhar would follow his own logic and give you half an hour, but of course, because he had a wicked sense of humour, he would invariably give you an hour's PS – Punishment School, or, at any other educational institution, detention. But that, basically, was how the exchange would go, in front of the whole class, naturally, who would gain as much pleasure and enjoyment from it as you would expect of teenage boys when one of their number is singled out for humiliation.

Peter Anthony Scott Farquhar – better known among my peers as Spine – taught English at Manchester Grammar School between 1970 and 1982. He taught me in 3T and 4T in the run-up to English language O-level, in which, a little disappointingly, I achieved a B. (Later, briefly, I had him for a sixth-form option in, possibly, philosophy, or was that Mr Leverton? It was all a long time ago.) Mr Farquhar would hand out detentions like they were sweets and no one would disagree that he was the most feared master in the school, despite the fact he never deployed a slipper or threw the board rubber across the room. A shortish, thin figure, a jacket on a backbone, he could be mistaken, as he walked ahead of you down the corridor carrying his leather briefcase, for a prefect. Indeed, a legend persists that one unfortunate boy ran the full length of the corridor to jump on Mr Farquhar's back, thinking him a sixth former.

The boy was rumoured to have received, as punishment for this ill-judged act, a whole term of Saturday Mornings.

With sixth-formers, however, Mr Farquhar was different. He addressed you as an equal, made you feel like a young man. In isolated cases, this could happen lower down the school, too. My friend Nigel Kendall was in his second year when Mr Farquhar encouraged him to write sarcastically, or ironically, because he said he had a good ear for the rhythm of a joke. Another 3T/4T classmate, Richard Little, adds, 'With the benefit of hindsight, plus thirty-seven years' marriage to an excellent secondary school teacher, I appreciate what a superb teacher he was. When I entered 3T, I was in the lower quartile for English in our year group of 210 boys. By the time I left 4T, I was in the upper quartile. Over those two years, he changed my views on English from a subject that had to be endured and passed at O-level (in order to progress on to Uni) into a subject that (dare I admit) I actually quite enjoyed. He did this by motivating me to try my hardest through thought-provoking lessons and copious amounts of encouragement. I will always remember studying Chaucer with him, especially because of the frequent references to "hogge torde" which appealed to my lavatorial 14-year-old mind. He showed us the linkage between the four languages we studied (French, German, English and Latin), which intrigued me. He was a firm but fair teacher – it was definitely best not to cross him.'

Other classmates from 3T and 4T remember more firmness than fairness and confess to mixed feelings, but all, of course, express shock and horror at what happened later. After leaving MGS, Mr Farquhar taught at Stowe School from 1983 to 2004, and from 2007 at the University of Buckingham, where he met student Ben Field, who was to become not only his friend and lover, but also his murderer. The story was turned, with great skill and sensitivity, into a BBC1 drama, *The Sixth Commandment*, written by Sarah Phelps and directed by Saul Dibb, the part of Farquhar played by Timothy Spall.

In the drama, broadcast in July 2023, Field and his friend Martyn Smith help Farquhar to get his first novel, *A Wide Wide Sea*, published, glossing over the fact that, while *A Wide Wide Sea* was the first novel Farquhar had written, he had already self-published two novels that he wrote subsequently, *Between Boy and Man* and *A Bitter Heart*.

I chose to read *A Bitter Heart*, as it is considerably shorter than *Between Boy and Man*. I wanted to like it more than I did. Mr Farquhar, as I still think of him, writes vividly about cold, damp, winter Manchester mornings – 'The drizzle was so fine that people were not always certain whether it was there or not . . . The exhaust fumes from the congested traffic could not escape into the atmosphere. A slimy patina stuck to the pavements. Lights stayed on all day. The last chrysanthemums withered on their stalks in suburban gardens' – but there are some problems with the novel at the level of character, dialogue and structure.

David Miller wrote to the letters page of the *TLS* from Chigwell, Essex, to draw our attention to similarities between the plot and the real-life story of what Field did to Farquhar. 'The book describes a church service in which the visiting preacher gives a lengthy sermon extolling the virtue of forgiveness. This mirrors a sermon Field gave at his father's church while on bail. The plan concocted by one of the characters slowly to poison the man she blames for her daughter's death similarly mirrors Field's real-life poisoning of Farquhar. That character, Mara, ultimately takes her own life by means of a drug overdose washed down with vodka, despite not being a regular drinker. Farquhar was not a habitual drinker either, but was suffocated by Field, who had laced his food and drink with substantial quantities of drugs, rendering him incapable of resisting attack. We may never know if Field read the novel and was inspired to use it as a blueprint for his plan to commit murder, or whether he made plot suggestions to the author as a device to hide in plain sight, but there are too many similarities between the novel and real life for comfort.'

Peter Anthony Scott Farquhar,
3 January 1946 – 26 October 2015.

Elizabeth Young's stories tended to come at the end of anthologies, whether because they were the best in the book, or they were often about endings, or editors thought, 'How do you follow that?', I don't know. Well, a bit of all three, I think, as sometimes I was the editor trying to make that decision.

I only have one clear memory of meeting Liz Young, which took place in her home in west London. I remember a first-floor flat on the west side of Ladbroke Grove, towards the top end, not far from the canal. Did I look through scaffolding, when I peered out at the traffic on the road below? A vague sense. An occluded view. Not that clear then. But I remember Liz's extraordinary, moon-white face. Her friend John Williams described her strong look – in a *Guardian* obituary – as 'Miss Havisham goes goth'.

Were we discussing work in progress? Whether we were or we weren't, I remember Liz's kindness, her making me feel at ease, when her shyness made it as difficult for her to meet people as I found it, too.

Then, an even more uncertain memory. Sitting in the back of a car being driven north up Ladbroke Grove. Was it Liz's car? I can't imagine Liz having a car, definitely not driving. Was it her husband Pete Mannheim's? Was Pete driving? Where were we going? Who else was in the car? Why was I there? Were they giving me a lift to the tube? But the tube was a short walk south of their flat. Were they taking me to Kensal Rise? This was before the London Overground, when no one used the North London Line if there was an alternative.

I first came across Liz when she wrote a very generous review in *City Limits* of *Darklands*, a small-press anthology of horror stories I had edited in 1991. Did I send her flowers, as I did to Anne Billson, for her review in the *Times*? I was young, I was naïve, but I was also overflowing with gratitude that needed to find some form of expression, however awkward. These intelligent, discerning critics didn't have to review my small-press effort. Certainly, no literary editor would have been leaning on them to do so. A year later, four days before I was due to send *Darklands 2* to the printer, a fax arrived, in the middle of the night. It was a short story submission. 'Lethality' by Elizabeth Young. It was incredible. If it had been a week later, I would have pulped the books and started again.

Elizabeth Young, born in Lagos, Nigeria, grew up under the dual influences of West African animist religions and the Free Presbyterianism of her Scottish parents. She attended a Quaker boarding school in York, and, after a year at the Sorbonne, went to York University to study contemporary American literature. On leaving university she went to London at the beginning of the punk era and worked as a fiction buyer in Compendium bookshop in Camden Town.

Later she would become widely published as a literary critic and feature writer, as enthusiastic about genre fiction as she was about the US writers she covered in *Shopping in Space: Essays on American 'Blank Generation' Fiction*, which she co-authored with Graham Caveney. Horror fiction, she believed, 'arises out of pity as much as fear, and writing it is a way to render bearable that which is psychically unendurable'. More of her critical writing was collected in *Pandora's Handbag: Adventures in the Book World*, which Serpent's Tail published posthumously.

Another posthumous publication is long overdue: a collection of her short stories, of which there are at least eight outstanding, substantial examples. She described two of them – 'Mother Can Take It' and 'The Garden of Eden Rainwear Catalogue' – as memoir, but published them in anthologies of short fiction; they work as either, or both. She wrote with astonishing frankness about drug use and sexual abuse, about outsiders and bullied individuals who refuse to become victims, always with a level of empathy and intelligence that left you in no doubt as to whose side she was on, and whose side you should be on, too.

The only trouble is, whoever has the job of assembling the contents of her collection, those stories can't all come last.

Elizabeth Jesse Young,
6 June 1950 – 18 March 2001.

A is for *A to Z*. I've got two Birmingham *A–Z*s. A colour one dated 1991 and a black and white one from three years earlier. It's this one that has one of Joel's old addresses written inside, in my handwriting, on the inside front cover: 739 Warwick Road. On the facing page, the contents page, written at the top, again in my handwriting, Joel's mobile number: 07909 627469. I sent a text to this number on Wednesday morning last week, to see who would answer, explaining who the number used to belong to. As of this morning, nobody has replied. On the last page of the *A–Z*, a blank page facing the inside back cover, in my handwriting again, in dark green felt tip, are a number of addresses – 567 Bristol Road, B29; 508 Bristol Road, B29; 232 & 230 Warwick Road, Greet, B11; Maxwells, 22 Shaftmoor Lane, Acock's Green, B27; 6 College Road, Quinton, B32; 189 High Street, Harborne, B17. I have no idea what they relate to. My best guess would be second-hand bookshops or balti houses, but Streetview doesn't offer up any evidence to support either hypothesis. According to the fictitious discography at the end of Joel's first novel, *From Blue to Black* (originally published by Serpent's Tail in 2000), Blue Away's album *Midnight Beat* was released in 1990 on A–Z Records.

B is for Blue. Joel Lane wrote three novels – *From Blue to Black*, *The Blue Mask*, and *Blue Midnight*, which was unpublished and was later retitled *The Missing Tracks*. He also wrote three stories called 'Blue Smoke', 'Blue Train' and 'Blue Mirror'. Believe it or not, there were also three poems: 'Blue Morning', 'Blue Town' and 'Blue Movie'. Influx Press will publish *Blue Midnight*, reinstating its original title.

C is for crime. Joel co-edited (with Steve Bishop) an original anthology, *Birmingham Noir*, published by Tindal Street Press in 2002. He also published a mini collection of crime stories, *Do Not Pass Go*, with Nine Arches Press in 2011, and for some readers his 2012 collection, *Where Furnaces Burn* (PS Publishing), his 'weird police stories', as he called them, was his best.

D is for Digbeth. When we were doing a photo shoot for the original edition of *The Earth Wire*, published by Egerton Press in 1994, I came to Birmingham and Joel took me around Digbeth and on to various canal tow paths. Three decades on, Birmingham has changed a bit.

E is for *The Earth Wire*, Joel's first collection. I can't remember if it was his idea or mine to publish a collection and nor can I remember how many I printed, probably 200. They didn't take long to sell out. When Influx Press asked if I had a digital version, I tried to open my old QuarkXpress file and couldn't. I know, I thought, I'll ask that nice small independent press that specialise in ghost stories and with whom I'd worked on a collection of stories by John Burke. I had agreed, as Joel's agent, at some point after Joel's death, I think, that they could publish an ebook version of *The Earth Wire*. Therefore, they would have a digital file. I asked the publisher if he had such a file and would let me have it. He agreed but for some reason didn't send it. Some months went by and Influx asked after the file again. I asked the man at the small independent press if he could send it. 'How much are you offering to pay?' he asked. Nothing, I said. This is a book I let you make available as an ebook, a book by our late friend, which another small independent is looking to reissue, to stimulate interest in his work, his reputation having grown since his death. 'But why should I let you have it for free?' he asked again. I tell this story because while most people in this business are nice people, good people, you shouldn't be too surprised if occasionally you come across someone who isn't.

F is for 'The Foggy, Foggy Dew'. Mark Valentine published Joel's story 'The Foggy, Foggy Dew' as a chapbook in 1986. As well as being a brilliant story, it was my introduction to the chapbook as a format for publishing a single short story, one that I would use some years later when I set up Nightjar Press and one of our first four titles was a new story by Joel called 'Black Country'.

G is for Gorey, Edward Gorey. Joel was a fan and, when he gave me a facsimile edition of Gorey's 1953 novel *The Unstrung Harp*, or *Mr Earbrass Write a Novel*, I became one too.

H is for Harrison, M John Harrison, who told me that Joel was the only writer whose talent he envied.

I is for In Memoriam: Chris Monk, a page on the internet site Flickr. Chris Monk, aka trav28, a friend of Joel's, did the cover illustration for Joel's Nightjar story, 'Black Country'. You can enjoy Chris's photographs, many of them featuring his wife Linda looking fabulous in a glossy black catsuit, online.

J is for Julie, an ex-girlfriend who, when I broke up with her, told me she'd only been pretending to like Joel's work. He was not a good writer, she told me. It was the final confirmation that I had been right to end the relationship.

K is for Keith, an ex-partner of Joel's. They lived together in Handsworth and were very kind to me when I needed emergency accommodation because of a personal matter involving Julie. Keith was a big Mike Oldfield fan and as a result of those intense few days I can't hear the opening tracks from Oldfield's 1991 album *Heaven's Open* without feeling a rush of excitement that soon veers off the road into traumatic memories of fear and anxiety.

L is for Leamington Spa. Most of Joel's stories were set in Birmingham or the Black Country, but there were a few exceptions, such as 'After the Flood', the opening story in *The Terrible Changes*, a hard-to-find collection published by Ex Occidente Press that, Joel wrote, in his introduction, 'tends towards the more low-key and private side of [his] writing'. After a flood in Leamington, Matthew's girlfriend Karen disappears. He meets another woman, an archivist, who reminds him of Karen. Re-reading this story yesterday I felt that swirling in its rich soup of influences I could glimpse William Sansom and HP Lovecraft, in the same image – 'Then the arm lifted towards him, coiling. It seemed to have no bones. It was hardly an arm at all' – and it occurred to me that had he been able to read any, Joel would have liked the stories of Birmingham-based library archivist Meave Haughey. The way in which Haughey writes about water in her story 'The Reservoir' reminds me of Joel's approach in 'After the Flood' and many other stories.

M is for Miserablism. In the late 1980s and early 1990s, a small group of writers became known as the Miserablists. The group comprised Joel, Conrad Williams, Christopher Kenworthy, Michael Marshall Smith, Graham Joyce and me. To be honest, Graham was an outlier and probably wouldn't have counted himself in. We were miserable because we didn't have girlfriends

– or boyfriends. In fact we weren't really miserable at all, especially Joel, who was easily the funniest member of the group, when he got going, but we were fed up with our day jobs and successive Tory governments and all we wanted to do was write horror stories. I think it was Christopher Fowler who first used the word in print to describe us, or some of us, or perhaps just one of us. We embraced the term and tried to exploit it for all it was worth. It didn't work.

N is for Nightingales. I think they're known as Nightingales, rather than The Nightingales, but they probably end up getting called The Nightingales, like Buzzcocks end up getting called The Buzzcocks. Joel was a fan of this Birmingham band – Nightingales – and he gave me their 2006 album *Out of True*, which I listen to quite a bit. They remind me more of The Fall than of Buzzcocks. And it's definitely The Fall, not Fall.

O is for Oakey, John Oakey, aka John Oakey Design, a very good friend of mine from when we both worked at Time Out. The first time we worked together outside of Time Out was on the original edition of *The Earth Wire*. John later very kindly agreed to be Nightjar's designer for nothing more than the occasional box of books and invitation to dinner.

P is for poetry. Joel won an Eric Gregory Award for his. I confessed to him that I didn't really get poetry, didn't understand it, didn't know what the point of it was. His response was to invite me to an event where he was reading his poetry. It did make more sense seeing and hearing the poet reading it.

Q is for 'Quarantine', a story in *Where Furnaces Burn* that is full of unanswered questions, as short stories should be. It includes a character called DC Morgan, no doubt named after Joel's friends Chris and Pauline Morgan. It's also full of great ideas/jokes, such as the police taking a building in for questioning, and powerful images – 'I saw tissue cultures on the walls of abandoned buildings. And lice creeping everywhere, as if the city had a skin' – and there's a line that reminds me of the most frightening experience I ever had in Joel's company. The line, in spite of the fact that the character being assisted by the narrator died in a locked hostel room a year earlier, seems harmless – 'Somehow, I got him moving along the road again. It was raining hard. There was no traffic in sight.' The episode it reminds me of took place in the early 1990s when Joel and I went to the Bush Theatre in Shepherd's Bush to see a production of a play by Richard Cameron. At some point during the performance, Joel seemed to withdraw, so that if I whispered a remark to him, he wouldn't acknowledge it. When the lights went up, he remained uncommunicative and I had to encourage him to leave the theatre – and indeed to make it to the tube, across London, and out of the Underground at Manor House, where we had a walk of about a mile along Seven Sisters Road. It wasn't raining, unlike in the story, but Joel required my assistance to walk, and there was traffic on the road. Indeed, a car filled with unfriendly-looking young men drew alongside and a door was opened. I pulled Joel into the road and somehow we got across four lanes to the other side and relative safety. Throughout the whole journey I had been repeatedly asking Joel if he was all right, telling him I didn't know what was going on and getting increasingly panicky. He would just stare blankly at me. Back at my flat, I offered him a biscuit and it was like magic. Suddenly, Joel was back in the room and he explained to me about diabetes and hypoglycaemia. I suggested he always carry biscuits in future.

R is for Ronnie Scott, the famous jazz tenor saxophonist and jazz club owner, who was Joel's uncle.

S is for Selly Oak. Joel lived there at 42 Lodge Hill Road.

T is for Tom. How lovely it is that Joel's brother Tom is here today.

U is for *Unspoken Water* and all the other small press journals and magazines where many of Joel's stories first appeared, including *Black Static*, *Postscripts*, *The Third Alternative*, *BFS Journal*, *Dark Horizons*, *Panurge*, *Critical Quarterly*, *Ambit*, *Maelstrom*, *Nutshell*, *Winter Chills*, *Dark Dreams*, *Skeleton Crew*, *Exuberance*, *Dementia 13*, *Roadworks*, *Supernatural Tales*, *Crimewave*, *New Horizons*, *Fusing Horizons*, *Under the Radar*, *Midnight Street*, *Peeping Tom*, *The Urbanite* and many more. Apologies to any I've omitted.

V is for Vitraea. When Jake asks Lang, in 'The Country of Glass', if he's heard of a place called Vitraea, it 'didn't so much ring a bell as strike a bass chord somewhere underground, causing reverberations in parts of his memory he didn't know were there'. It also kicks off a search for this fabled land, which Lang calls the country of glass and which will remind the reader of M John Harrison's Egnaro in the story of the same name. 'The Country of Glass' is one of Joel's strongest and bleakest stories. Anyone who's not read it will both want a drink and not want a drink after reading it.

W is for the Wren's Nest, a Black Country beauty spot that featured in more than one story in *Where Furnaces Burn*.

X is for X. No, not Elon Musk's shabby version of Twitter, which Joel would have hated, but the single kiss he – Joel, that is – added to each of the dedications he wrote to me in copies of his books, except for *From Blue to Black*, in which, for some reason, there are three.

Y is for Yardley Wood, another one of the many names of districts in Birmingham and the West Midlands that have extra resonance for me as places where Joel lived and from where he would send me long, detailed letters full of very generous feedback about my stories. He would write in black on lined paper, with small, careful handwriting. I suspect a lot of people received such letters. Joel was a friend to many and had many friends. Many of them are here today. If *he* were here today, he'd say, 'Hi, how're things with you?'

Z is for zombie. I'm scraping the barrel here, but in *The Witnesses Are Gone*, there's a line, 'The sky was the blue of a Romero zombie.' And in *Midnight Blue*, there's another line: 'Oak and beech trees reached from the crumbling reddish ground like zombies in a graveyard.' The truth is that Joel didn't really write zombie stories, even though a lot of his characters would sometimes inhabit zombie-like states, and nor is there much or anything else starting with a Z, as far as I can see and I've been scouring his work over the last few days – a great pleasure, it must be said. It's almost as if, Joel's sense of humour being what it was, he planned it this way, so that any individual attempting a Joel Lane alphabet approach to a talk like this, at the start of a day-long symposium devoted to the man and his work, would end up looking a fool.

Joel David Mandela Lane,
2 October 1963 – 26 November 2013.

8

Mike Nelson's books

There may be fewer rooms in installation artist Mike Nelson's 2022 show, *The Book of Spells (A Speculative Fiction)*, than in much of his previous work, but there are more books.

My first encounter with Nelson's work set up certain expectations. In 2000, Nelson transformed Matt's Gallery, creating a series of rooms, an immersive promenade, or perhaps something closer to a ghost-train ride or a film, but a film in which *you* move through *it* rather than having *it* move through *you*. If the mind has a fuse, *The Coral Reef* blew it.

In my memories of *The Coral Reef* – both at Matt's Gallery and later at Tate Britain – its rooms are full of books, but when I check this with Nelson, he says there were 'only one or two Marxist treatises in the Mexican revolutionaries room'. Maybe Jonathan Jones' words in the *Guardian* had sunk in – '*The Coral Reef* is the installation as scary novel' – or I had spent too long looking at the pictures in *Extinction Beckons* (Matt's Gallery, 2000), but at some point I had created a picture in my mind of Nelson sneaking into his own installations to leave books lying around like props. They might be dropped singly under a hammock (*Agent Dickson at the Red Star Hotel*, Hales Gallery,

London, 1995) or splayed on the floor next to a dog's bowl (*Trading Station Alpha Cma*, Matt's Gallery, London, 1996) or be dumped in bundles tied with twine (*Lionheart*, Galerie im Künstlerhaus, Bremen, 1997).

Jonathan Jones isn't the only critic to have highlighted Nelson's enthusiasm for books. Writing about Nelson's 2004 show *Triple Bluff Canyon* in the *Independent on Sunday*, Charles Darwent refers to the artist's 'literary cleverness', and in a piece in the *Guardian* about Nelson's contribution to the 2011 Venice biennale, Rachel Withers writes: '*The Coral Reef*'s duplicated room isn't just about giving visitors a frisson. It feels like a literary device, like something out of Borges. It signals Nelson's passion for literature, not least for genre fiction with its recurring characters and plot devices and its skewed relationship to the real.' She adds, 'When we "read" Nelson's installation we're invited to let our sense of its authorship, its authenticity, slip and slide in a quasi-literary fashion.'

In the shows leading up to *The Coral Reef*, there was hardly one that didn't feature at least one book, and in more recent pieces, books are increasingly the point. Hundreds are included, even if we can't see them, in *An Invocation: Five Hundred and Thirty Books From Southend Central Library* (2013), salvaged from the demolished bibliotheca and packed into the cavity wall of the gallery built in its place. Hundreds more – travel guides from Lonely Planet, Rough Guides, Time Out – fill the shelves of the single person's bedroom that is *The Book of Spells* and not only may we gaze upon them, but, as if this were the second-hand bookshop it feels like to me, we may handle them, flick through them, smell the pages, look for names of former owners, such as Mrs R Myhill of Cirencester with her damaged-in-transit bargain-priced copy of the *Time Out London Guide*, earlier editions of which I was lucky enough to edit decades ago. On a high shelf, out of reach, are two copies of the *Time Out Dublin Guide*, an early edition of which was also mine.

A week after resurfacing, enchanted, from my allotted fifteen minutes in *The Book of Spells*, I walk from Stoke Newington to Crystal Palace, reading, fittingly, HP Lovecraft's *The Call of Cthulhu*. Nelson's studio, concealed behind a former shop front, is arranged over three levels and is packed with heads, tools, cassettes, rolls of tape, cans of WD40 and lots and lots of books. It reminds me of *Triple Bluff Canyon* (Modern Art Oxford, 2004), which incorporated a reconstruction of the artist's then studio (and a great deal of sand). We have a vague plan to talk about books in his work, but our conversation, fuelled by Turkish tea and Tunnocks Wafer Biscuits, ranges over health anxiety, Central Books, artists from Ilya Kabakov to Paul Thek to Jim Whiting, and the 1930 tropical-hardwood bureau, which he shows me, that Nelson wrote about in his short story, 'On Monkeys Without Tails', in *The New Abject* edited by Sarah Eyre and Ra Page (2020, Comma Press).

'As a child I was slow to read,' Nelson tells me when we pick up the threads of our conversation later. 'My parents were impressed because I would spend hours looking at books but then they realised I was only looking at the pictures.' His reading career was 'jump-started' by *Watership Down*, which he read when he was eleven, and by the effect of feeling homesick on a French exchange two years later. 'I was quite literate in my midteens, then I dropped back out of it. At college I was reading the theory that was deemed useful and fashionable to read at the time, some of which stuck and some of which didn't. It wasn't until I left college that I started reading and I read a lot then, through my twenties, and that was a lot of fiction, because what

I found in fiction was a more soluble form of the theory that I'd read at college. Writers like Lem or Ballard, even going back to Conrad.

'I remember my tutor, Christine Angus, talking about the making of art, about the relationship between experience – the absorption of stimuli – and the actual *doing*. I left college. I did a lot of travelling. She said, "You've seen a lot. You need to make something now." I think, with the amount of fiction absorbed in the 1990s and early 2000s, I needed the time to compute it. There was only so much I could take in. I was lucky that I found a stream. It's a bit like gold mining. You find a stream of stuff that takes you somewhere. It was a particularly useful one for me in regard to where it led me.'

That stream flows directly into *The Forgotten Kingdom*, an anthology of reprinted stories and extracts that Nelson put together with Will Bradley to accompany his 2001 show at the ICA. Borges, Burroughs, Lem, Kafka, Lovecraft – they're all in there, and many others. 'It's a Frankenstein of a book,' Nelson says. 'I Frankensteined all these elements. Even the title is from another book.' The Kafka story was the only one that wasn't Nelson's choice. Kafka was expensive, and the longer the story the more it would cost, so Bradley suggested 'The Departure', a single, short paragraph. 'Actually,' says Nelson, 'it's a fantastic short story. I've got Will to thank for that. The idea of escape is so prevalent in those works. *The Coral Reef* was about escape and entrapment. It was a great pleasure to do that book with Will. I like the fact that even though it's disjointed you could almost read it like a traditional book, with chapters and frontispiece and postscripts. Obviously, it doesn't really make any sense, but if you know what I *do*, perhaps it does, somehow, or at least it makes sense to me.'

Bradley and Nelson would go down to the local second-hand bookshop in Balham, where Nelson was living at the time, and find copies of books by the authors they had agreed on. I wonder if this was the Oxfam Bookshop where, in 2017, I found a Penguin edition of Borges's *The Book of Imaginary Beings*, with Peter Goodfellow's Bosch-inspired cover and an inclusion in the form of a postcard, from Jen to Tony, reflecting on her recent performance as Doll in *Sir Thomas More*. But Nelson tells me the bookshop was called My Back Pages.

'It's gone, unfortunately. It's turned into another estate agent's, which pretty much sums Balham up.'

If it wasn't an estate agent's it would be a hairdresser's, but Nelson is right: it's an estate agent's. According to the London Bookshop Map, the owner of My Back Pages opened a new shop, Turn the Page, in Earlsfield in 2014, but that closed in 2016.

It was in 1994 that Nelson started using books in his work. His show *Charity Shop* changed the name of Transmission in Glasgow to Transmission Charity Shop. He bought a tent, for use in disaster situations, put it up in the 'charity shop' and brought in a stack of copies of an Oxfam publication, *Plastic Sheeting: Its Use For Emergency Shelter and Other Purposes*, which became the show's catalogue.

'At the time, it seemed quite clever, with a dark humour to it, but when I witnessed people walking in, I didn't feel they took the way of thinking to its conclusion. They just saw the thing, clocked it as contemporary art and that was kind of it. I was a little disappointed, but at the same time I'd built this piece called *Taylor*, which also consisted of a tent, on top of a raft made out of oil drums and these boxes on the back, with a stack of books, the top one of which was about Lenin, in Arabic, which I'd bought in Berlin many years ago, because it was such an intriguing object.'

The work was a response to the Haitian refugee crisis. 'It was made on the top floor of a Liverpool warehouse that overlooked the docks, an early nineteenth-century warehouse, so kind of the last bastion of the British slave trade. It seemed pertinent to make a cinematic or literary reference, this one to Charlton Heston's character in *Planet of the Apes*. He sets off to find a new world, only to find himself back in the same place, but in a worse situation. That was the first work where there was a literary or filmic reference and also books creeping in. When I watched people react to that, I found it much richer. That early work I'd describe as a prop from a non-existent film or I'd make a script from a reference to the site it was in, to the time that we were living in, a political event, then also to a literary or filmic *other* and then somehow make a residue from that process, which was the object, the raft, and then that would be a catalyst for the viewer, with their own baggage, their own histories, their own memories, to engage. I think that was the beginning of that way of working and it was a direct influence of literature, of reading.'

The copies of *Plastic Sheeting* had come from Central Books in Hackney Wick. 'My relationship to books,' Nelson tells me, 'was formed by Central Books. When I was at college, I got a job as a rep for various publishers including Serpent's Tail and also for all the old Soviet books and cultural theory books and God knows what. I moved downstairs from the offices at the top into the warehouse. I worked for several years on and off doing various jobs, sweeping up, shifting pallets, but also picking – picking orders. I loved that process of being sent, within this great Victorian warehouse over several floors and another building across the road, to, say, W39 X5 A41. It might be a book on queer art or Marx and Engels or a Semiotext(e)

volume or a piece of fiction. It could be *The Satanic Verses*. We
had huge pallets of *The Satanic Verses*.

'Even though you had to get the orders out, there was a bit of
time to stop and read, so you'd stop and have a rummage. I even
used to make maquettes for work in some of the back rooms
and do drawings on the boxes, trying to work out ideas. There
were a few other artists – Dave Beech, Dave Burrows – and it
formed the way I thought of books in terms of their essence as
an object. I've always enjoyed the *communication* of a book, in
its essence, without even opening it up.

'The other day I picked up a copy of Wilfred Thesiger's
Arabian Sands, a really early copy, outside the BFI. I'm working
on a show at the Hayward Gallery and I'm thinking of reshow-
ing *Triple Bluff Canyon*, with all the sand, and it seemed pertinent that this book had somehow landed.'

For Nelson, everything is connected. He may appear to jump
from one subject to another, but there's always a through line.

'People wonder about the use of libraries if nobody ever goes
in them,' he says. 'Actually people do go in them, but even if
they don't, the potential to go in them is there, and the library's
existence as a piece of architecture signifies that potential and,
even if you don't ever go in, it imbues the populace with an
intelligence and a knowledge. I think the same thing happens
with books. They kind of bear witness, don't they, when they sit
on a shelf, at the end of your bed, next to you? They're entities
and they come not only with the histories and the knowledge
and the intent of the people that write them, but also, especially with second-hand books, those that have handled and read
them before. This might sound a little fanciful, but I enjoy that
potential.'

It doesn't sound fanciful to me. I will repeat it next time

someone asks me how many books in my collection I've actually read.

'That's very much what *The Book of Spells* was touching on as well,' Nelson continues, 'in terms of all these travel guides that may have visited all these places and then come back. To bring them all together is like the construction of a shrine, the layering of the powers of these objects and their histories and their owners' histories.'

I admit, silently, that I want to go back to Matt's Gallery with a set of library steps to allow me to reach that high shelf and see if it was my edition of the *Time Out Dublin Guide* or a later one. Then I'd lie down on the single bed in the middle of the room and just enjoy looking at all the spines of all those books all around me. Trapped, enclosed, isolated, but with the potential for at least imagined escape.

Tuesday 3 October 2023
Oxfam Books & Music, Crouch End, London.
Little boy in blue school uniform: Have you got any Bunny vs Monkey books?
Volunteer: Pardon?
Boy: Have you got any Bunny vs Monkey books?
Volunteer: I don't know is the only answer I can give you. If you have a look in the children's section, which is just down there, you'll be able to see if we have. We just have contributions, you see. You could ask the manager, who's just in there. His name is Greg.
Boy [moving to doorway to office]: Have you got any Bunny vs Monkey books?
Greg [exiting office]: Pardon?
Boy: Have you got any Bunny vs Monkey books?

Greg: Are they a series of books? Do you know who they're by?

Boy: Jamie Smart, I think.

Greg [having a look]: It doesn't look like we do, but you did the right thing by asking. If you can pop in again, just ask again.

The show at the Hayward Gallery that Nelson refers to in our conversation above ran from 22 February to 7 May 2023. *Extinction Beckons* was billed as 'the first major survey of work' by the internationally acclaimed British artist, who has represented Britain at the Venice Biennale (in 2011) and twice been nominated for the Turner Prize (in 2001 and 2007). It featured, among the discrete installations that formed the show, a number of books. In the largest piece, *The Deliverance and the Patience*, a huge labyrinth of rooms, stairs, doors and corridors that couldn't fail to remind Nelson fans of *The Coral Reef*, we came across an extremely well-thumbed Autonomedia edition of *T. A. Z.: The Temporary Autonomous Zone* by the anarchist writer and poet Hakim Bey (Peter Lamborn Wilson), while the smallest work, a recreation of the artist's former studio, was stuffed with books.

Lying flat on the worktop was a hardback copy of *Conrad and His World* (Thames & Hudson) by Norman Sherry – 'with 142 illustrations'. Partially overlapping Sherry's book and itself supporting a roll of duct tape was a copy of the 1991 Calder Publications paperback edition of Borges's *Fictions* with a cover design by Thomi Wroblewski. My copy of this edition, which I found in the Jambala Buddhist charity bookshop in Bethnal Green in January 2023, has a note written on the flyleaf in ballpoint pen: 'The Slade, Gower Street. Near Euston Sq tube on the mid left side by benches.' On a blank page at the back of the book, in the same handwriting, are some workings-out and a diagram relating to the fable of the Tortoise and the Hare.

The writer's conclusion: 'Thus the hare would not overtake the tortoise!!' Whether there might be any connection with Borges's collection of essays *The Perpetual Race of Achilles and the Tortoise* is unclear.

There were two thick books called *Magazine*, also on the worktop, and a 1973 New English Library edition of Doug Lang's novel *Freaks*. Lying next to a lethal-looking animal horn was a US paperback edition from Airmont of Jules Verne's *A Journey to the Center of the Earth*. We could see a Taschen hardback, *Art Now*, lying on top of some yellow volumes, next to a couple of hefty encyclopaedic tomes, and let that be the only use of the word 'tome' in this book. Apart from that one. The old edition of Wilfred Thesiger's *Arabian Sands* that Nelson mentions above, which he found on the book tables outside the BFI, under Waterloo Bridge, lying on top of another unjacketed hardback, *Taxidermy* by Leon L Pray. Underneath these, on an actual bookshelf: Dennis Cooper's *Try* (Serpent's Tail), Christina Stead's *Cotters' England* (Virago Modern Classics) and unidentified titles by Elizabeth Bowen and Julian Barnes.

9

Home again, home again

On a Sunday in August 2023 I walked down from Stoke Newington to Spitalfields to hand-deliver a Nightjar order to an address in one of the low-rise blocks on the Middlesex Street Estate, built for the Corporation of London between 1965 and 1970. I couldn't gain access to the complex at the appropriate entry point, despite trying several different flats, including the one written on the address label, so I went around the corner and tried a different entrance where there was a hand-written notice on the door saying, 'Life Drawing, BUZZ 101 CALL, 1st Floor in Lift.' I tried a couple of flats, hoping that if someone were to buzz me in, I might be able to find my way to the address I needed.

Finally, I tried 101, wondering if I had actually wanted the other calls to remain unanswered.

It was answered immediately and I started saying something about a delivery, but a woman's voice cut across me: 'First floor, in the lift.' I pulled open the door and took the lift past the first floor to the sixth floor, where I enjoyed great views both towards the City and over east London. I delivered my Nightjar order and left. Curious though I am about life drawing, I decided I had enough going on.

In the second-hand basement at Burley Fisher Books, on the walk back to Stoke Newington, I found the copy of Zola's *Nana* (Penguin Classics) with its inclusion at page 327, a receipt, dated 24 February, for an order of travel cheques in the name of Emma Chichester-Clark, already mentioned in another chapter, or not yet mentioned, depending on the order in which, at the last minute, I decide to put things. I also bought *The Vintage Turgenev Volume 2* with a dedication on the flyleaf: 'In deep appreciation of my stay with the Pratt family which has made London a warm and friendly place, Ian Anderson.' At page 177 there was a torn-off corner from a piece of letterhead from the London School of Economics (LSE) with an 071 phone number, meaning it dated from between 1990 and 1995.

It was a US edition of Turgenev, so I imagined that Ian Anderson was American and brought the book with him to give as a present to his hosts, the Pratt family. Later, I'm guessing a member of the Pratt family was reading the book and needed a bookmark. Seeing before him or her, on the desk, a letter from the LSE, he or she tore off the corner and slipped it in at page 177. I decided to write to the librarians at the LSE and see if they would accept the book as a donation and place it in their stock.

The following day, walking from Stoke Newington to the LSE, I stopped off first at Oxfam Dalston – well, it would be weird not to – where I bought a duplicate copy of the lovely Virago Modern Classics edition of Charlotte Perkins Gilman's *The Yellow Wallpaper*, thinking I might give it away in a Nightjar offer, and *Storia 3: Consequences* (Pandora), which has stories in it by Rebecca Brown, Eva Figes and others. I had read Rebecca Brown's 1990 Picador collection, *The Terrible Girls*, the summer before and loved it, especially the penultimate story, 'What I

Did', which begins, 'My job was to carry the bag.' What was in the bag? Do we want to know? Well, yes and no.

In the House of Grace charity shop further down Kingsland Road, I found *The Penguin Guide to London* by FR Banks, with a tube map inclusion at page 241. I bought it for a project I had thought at one point might become part of this book, but now I am thinking it will be part of the next book, as long as this book doesn't become the enormous failure every writer who doesn't have an 'ego room' fears all of their books will become.

At LSE, I was able to deliver the Turgenev to the Library desk and then email Nancy Graham, Associate Director, Collections and Academic Services, who got back to me only an hour or so later to thank me and say she would accept the book into the Main Collection. Not only did the Library have a number of collections on Russia, she wrote, but students were often asking them to buy more fiction. Nancy said that she would ask the cataloguing team to include a note on the record to say that I had kindly donated the book and she said that she would also ask them to attach the corner of the letter to the inside cover. She went on: 'You wouldn't believe the fascinating things we find tucked inside books, left by students and other readers.' When working at King's College London some years ago, Nancy told me, she found a letter from Surrey Police advising the addressee that they could go to a local police station to collect their confiscated shotgun. She added that when she had opened my email she had recognised my name from reading my first novel, *Counterparts*, many years ago.

I may not have an 'ego room', but I must admit to possessing an ego, and it felt gently burnished by that. But then I realised I was also more than a little surprised that someone who had recognised my name from reading *Counterparts* should then open and read my email rather than immediately delete it.

As if Nancy hadn't already done enough to indulge me, she then went on to say that she had done a little research of her own and discovered that there was an academic by the name of Pratt at another institution who worked at the LSE during the years when it had an 071 phone number. A possible connection there? I emailed this individual a while later and have not yet had a reply, but I remember only too well what it's like having a university email inbox. It fills up mostly with emails you don't want to open, emails from senior management advising you of pointless changes to ways of working that have worked perfectly well for years, or of your required attendance at training seminars in regard to procedures you don't really need to be trained in, or, well, you can imagine. I mean, it might be an email from the Head of Research inviting you to pop along and see him to have that conversation about your request for promotion, so you do pop along and you tell him you're interested in applying for promotion from Senior Lecturer to Professor and he laughs in your face and says, 'Reader, possibly,' and then years later, when you're only a year away from leaving the job altogether, having achieved the Readership some years earlier, you pop along to Bopcap Books in Levenshulme and find a copy of Patrick Gale's *Little Bits of Baby* with the name of the now former Head of Research written on the title page in ballpoint pen along with the date, 1st March 93, and because it's a Paladin, and you are collecting Paladins, you buy it.

It would be nice to be able to report that *Little Bits of Baby* contained some embarrassing inclusion, libellous gossip about a former colleague, perhaps, or a receipt for a subscription to *Elevator World: The Magazine of the International Building Transportation Industry*, but there was nothing, not a sausage, not even a coffee stirrer (which is fast becoming one of the most commonly found inclusions in second-hand books), and this is a non-fiction book, so nothing in it is made up.

An academic who did reply to an email was Dr Rhodri Hayward, Reader in History at Queen Mary College, University of London, where I studied languages, and founder member of the Centre for the History of the Emotions. I had found, on Wednesday 15 February 2023 in the Amnesty Bookshop in Kentish Town, a copy of Mick Jackson's Booker Prize-shortlisted novel *The Underground Man* (Picador) with Dr Hayward's beautiful bookplate on the inside front cover and an appropriate and very funny cutting from *Private Eye* about a Russian pensioner who had embarked on a solo project of digging a metro system for his home town pasted onto the inside back cover. I emailed Dr Hayward and he kindly replied, explaining that he often grangerises books as he finds it's a good way to get rid of old papers. I was very pleased to be introduced to a new word that I should perhaps have already been familiar with.

Tuesday 2 October 2018
Looking around a second-hand CD/book dealer's place. His stuff was laid out in a not very salubrious car park at the rear of a property. On my visit, it was mainly CDs. My feeling was that sometimes he had more books. I picked out a big, thick French novel in Livres de Poche. Red cover, cracked spine. Author's name didn't sound French. Title was *O2*, like the phone company, but the edition pre-dated the phone company. I found it had an inclusion – a little photo or bit of paper with dried earwigs stuck on that I was trying to brush off, with mixed success. I'd get one insect or bit of dirt off, then notice another.

In May 2022 I was reading Sam Lipsyte's short story collection *Venus Drive*, which I'd bought the month before from Oxfam Dalston along with W Somerset Maugham's *Collected Short Stories Vol 3* (Penguin), which I knew I probably already had, but this copy, while tatty, did have a receipt in it, dated 13 August 1983, for lessons at the French Cultural Centre in Khartoum, paid for by Samia Omar Osman. The receipt was tucked inside the back cover, and there were two names written on the flyleaf, Ann and Amin, and a four-digit number.

I think I wasn't in the right mood for *Venus Drive*, which the internet says is funny, if grimly funny, because I found it profoundly depressing. Was Lipsyte writing from experience, I wondered (I hoped not), or did he sneak in under the wire before it became the law that you must be part of whatever community you're writing about? I needed cheering up and managed to achieve that by visiting the Sue Ryder charity shop in Didsbury. (I was starting from quite a low point.) I don't often find much in Sue Ryder, but every now and then they do get some good new (old) stuff in, like, on this occasion, *Girl Film & Television Annual 1961* (Long Acre Press), which I bought to give to my wife. What girl wouldn't want a copy of *Girl Film & Television Annual*? Clive Bell's *Civilization* (Pelican) to send to someone I know called Clive Bell. All right, *the* Clive Bell, the musician, composer and writer with a specialist interest in East Asian wind instruments. Because I was sure no one else had ever given him a book before by the other Clive Bell, who apparently was some sort of art critic and writer associated with the Bloomsbury Group.

And, if that wasn't enough, I also found a first edition of LTC Rolt's *The Inland Waterways of England* (Allen & Unwin), previously owned by Sylvia Grove of Market Harborough in August 1950. It even contained an inclusion, at page 87, a blank postcard of an aqueduct.

Best of all was a 1957 Penguin edition of Stanley Kauffmann's novel *The Philanderer* with an inclusion at page 35, a delivery note from Burton the tailor at 2–4 Gloucester Road, Bristol (now a Sainsbury's Local), dated 2/11/57 for a Mr Sutcliffe at an address in Kennington Avenue in the Bishopston district of Bristol.

A few weeks later, I sent the book, with its inclusion and a note explaining what I was doing, to the occupants of the Kennington Avenue address. It seemed to me that the book should perhaps have an opportunity to return to where it had once lived. Enough time – 65 years – had elapsed for it to be unlikely that Mr Sutcliffe or any of his descendants would still be living at the property, but books have long memories and this one, I thought, might want to go home.

A couple of weeks later I got a letter in the post from Matthew Thomas of Kennington Avenue thanking me for the book. He is a 'voracious reader', he wrote. He and his wife have lived at the address for many years, but not far back enough to have any knowledge of Mr Sutcliffe. Kennington Avenue is a long road linking Bishopston with Ashley Down. In 1957, Matthew wrote, there would have been four cars in the road. Now there are a great many more. Because of the location of their house they are able to enjoy a view of Gloucestershire's cricket matches, when they're not giving music tuition to students learning piano, flute, keyboard or electronic organ.

My first attempt at returning a book to its former home had gone well. Perhaps too well. I was spoilt. Now, I would expect engagement every time. I would expect a kind letter. Maybe an ongoing correspondence and lifelong friendship? To be reunited with someone I hadn't seen in half a century? Freedom of the city? Fellowship of the Royal Society of Literature? An OBE I would accept only because of how proud it would make my mum?

I needed to be brought back down to earth.

Luckily, real life has many ways of doing just that.

I gathered together some books that I had already acquired that had addresses in and looked long and hard at them to try to work out if I was ready to let them go.

I looked at the Picador edition of Salman Rushdie's *The Jaguar Smile* that I had found in Oxfam Bookshop Chorlton in July 2021. I'd already got a copy of that title, in my Picador collection, but this one had in it the name of a previous owner – Canon Graham Smith – and an address on Gorringe Park Avenue, Mitcham, Surrey.

I had a look at a lovely old Penguin Modern Classics edition of Katherine Mansfield's *Letters and Journals* previously owned by Alexander C Games, of Wembley, who I had decided might be the journalist Alex Games. I had bought it from Oxfam Shop Marylebone High Street in August 2021.

I considered a copy of DM Thomas's *The White Hotel* (King Penguin) with an inclusion in the form of a BIFF postcard party invitation. The party was at an address in Clonmell Road, London SW6. I had liberated the book from the excellent House of Hodge charity bookshop in Finsbury Park in February 2022.

Finally, could I really bear to part with the Penguin Modern Classics edition of Kafka's *The Trial* I'd bought from Greenhouse Books, Cheadle, in October 2021, with, at page 10, a postcard dated 15 June 1969 from historian RC Mowat of Highfield

Avenue, Oxford, to Isobel Beattie of Winchester Road, Oxford, bearing a 5d stamp, reminding her to invoice him for typing at 8 shillings per 1000 words?

Over the coming months I looked for and found more books containing old addresses. In a book sale at the University of Manchester Students' Union I found a copy of Alan Sillitoe's *The Loneliness of the Long-Distance Runner*, a Great Pan with a great inclusion inside the front cover, a postcard from Kendals department store dated 28 December 1966 advertising their January sale. It was addressed to Mr and Mrs N Kessel at an address on Lees Road, Bramhall. Inside the front cover also, in blue ballpoint, the name Valerie Kessel, and the date, 1962. In the Children's Society in Heaton Moor, Stockport, I found DH Lawrence's *The Virgin and the Gipsy* (Penguin) with an Austin Drive address, five minutes from where I live. On a later visit to the Children's Society, I came away with Evelyn Waugh's *Brideshead Revisited* (Penguin Modern Classics) with an inclusion, a pay slip from 2008. There was a name, of course, and an address in Farm Close, Heaton Chapel. (I easily resisted a hardback edition of *The Guts* by Roddy Doyle with a coffee stirrer for a bookmark. Unused. I think.)

It's a question of trying to gauge how long ago a book left the address that remains inside it. If it looks like it's just come straight from that address to the charity shop, then the last thing its former owner wants is to see it drop through their front door. Little printed white or gold address labels of a certain type are a dead giveaway. I don't know if you can still get them; you certainly don't see them much any more. My dad had some in the 1970s. I think everybody's dad did. If they have a phone number on and the phone number has a prefix that's been changed, that's a clue. Of course, people hang on to books for years, for decades, and may then get rid of them. It doesn't mean they've moved. But you make a judgment. You do some research, perhaps, and you make a judgment.

I decided in the case of the copy of *In Another Europe* (Sceptre) by Georgina Harding that I bought from my local Oxfam in December 2017 and that had one of those little address labels in it and gave the address as another flat in the same development as mine, that the named individual was probably long gone, so I wrote my little note, packaged it up and left it in the porch of the appropriate block. No response. I haven't seen it back in Oxfam, though, so there's that, at least.

A copy of Ian McEwan's *The Children Act* (Vintage) that I found in Oxfam Walthamstow in July 2022 had a good inclusion – a driving licence. It had belonged to a young man whose address I could walk to in less than one minute from my wife's flat, so one day I grabbed the book and did just that. For some reason I hadn't put it in an envelope and when I got there I knocked on his door, but there was no one in and because I hadn't put it in an envelope or written a note, I didn't post the book, because that really would be weird, wouldn't it? That would be like David Lynch's *Lost Highway*. Or Michael Haneke's *Hidden*. But with a book, with an old driving licence inside it, instead of a video cassette containing vaguely menacing videos.

I haven't tried again. I feel like that ship has sailed.

I posted Katherine Mansfield's *Letters and Journals* to the address in Wembley and *The White Hotel* to Clonmell Road, SW6. I popped *The Virgin and the Gipsy* through a letter box on Austin Drive and dropped *Brideshead Revisited* through the door of a quiet-looking bungalow in Heaton Chapel. I went on a long but not especially lonely walk to Bramhall to deliver Valerie

Kessel's copy of *The Loneliness of the Long-Distance Runner* to its former home in Lees Road.

There were others, but I didn't keep a full record. Maybe I was happy to forget about them once they'd gone – it sometimes seems to me that all I am really doing most of the time is moving books from one place to another, whether I'm keeping them or giving them away – or maybe I just wanted to be pleasantly surprised if anyone did get in touch ever again.

Monday 11 December 2023

Waterstone's, Deansgate, Manchester.

Customer [older woman browsing M shelf in fiction, holding book by Benjamin Myers]: You haven't got *The Offing*, have you?

Bookseller [checking device]: No, I'm afraid not. We've got it in our smaller stores. Wilmslow, Stockport, Altrincham, Bolton.

Customer: It's a lovely story. It stays in your mind. You don't want it to end. Read it!

Bookseller: I will. I'll take your recommendation. Thank you.

In August 2023, Oxfam Bookshop Chorlton got a load of Simenons in. The hardbacks went quickly. The Penguins hung around for longer. My friend Rae bought some. I bought some. They all had the same name in – Mike Stott or MA Stott– and a number of different addresses, mostly in London and one in Walsden, down the road from Todmorden, Lancashire, which as I'm sure you know is home to the excellent Lyall's second-hand bookshop. Mike Stott, I discovered, was a playwright – a 'Northern playwright' according to his *Guardian* obituary by Michael Coveney. To be fair to Coveney, the 'Northern playwright' detail is in the headline, which he would not have written – who died in 2009 at the age of 65 (Stott, not Coveney). A couple of paragraphs from Mike Leigh follow Michael Coveney's piece. Leigh adds, 'In 1967, Mike was assistant dramaturg to Jeremy Brooks at the RSC. I joined as assistant director, and we were both involved in Theatregoround, the company's new outreach set-up.' This explained the address that Stott had written in some of the Simenons – c/o RSC, Aldwych Theatre, WC2. There were also a couple of addresses in Clapham and the one in Walsden, where, according to the *Guardian*, he had settled in 1977. The London dates, in the books, in Stott's neat handwriting, ranged from 1967 to 1970.

On the last Friday in August I set out to walk from Stoke Newington to the Aldwych and then on to Clapham. Just as Mike Harding used to joke that he – or was it one of his characters? – couldn't walk past pubs, I can't walk past second-hand bookshops, which is how I ended up in Oxfam Dalston again. I know, I could go another way, but Kingsland Road, for a main road, is a strangely pleasant road to walk down, especially when the sun is out. They had – and now I have – another Patrick Gale. This one was *A Place Called Winter* (Tinder Press), with a very good inclusion at page 87, a card from a TV producer to a well-known actor. It's all very luvvie and I love it.

I had a stroke of luck when I reached the Aldwych Theatre. The theatre manager, Craig Nichols-Young, to whom I had addressed my note and the packaged-up copy of Simenon's *Account Unsettled*, was speaking to someone at the door of the theatre, so I waited for their conversation to finish and then handed him the package.

I headed down to Clapham. When I reached the address in Abbeville Road that Stott had written in his copy of *Maigret*

Meets a Milord, with the date November 1970, my timing was less good. The residents appeared to be in the middle of moving out. The front door was standing open, boxes everywhere. I placed the package on the hall floor and stepped away, then immediately thought it was a bad idea – I should come back when the new people had moved in – but it was too late to retrieve it. What if someone appeared at the moment of my bending down to pick it up? So I left, kicking myself, which is difficult while you're on the move, but it wasn't far to the next address in Klea Avenue where Stott had lived in March 1967. No obvious moving in or out there, although Stott had presumably had to move out between March and June, the date in the copy of *Account Unsettled* I had left at the Aldwych Theatre.

There's been no response from either Clapham address, but Craig Nichols-Young sends a lovely email thanking me for the book, which he photographed on a coffee table in his office alongside programmes returned to the theatre by the daughter of a customer who had passed away, including one for Jules Feiffer's *Little Murders*, an RSC production in the theatre in 1967. Staff were welcome to borrow the book and read it, Craig explained. The Aldwych Theatre, which was 118 years old on 23 December 2023, seems a well-run and happy place.

I get no responses from Wembley, Clonmell Road or Winchester Road in Oxford. Nothing from Austin Drive and resounding silence from Lees Road in Bramhall. No response either from the Principal Hotel in York after I email them to ask if the weather forecast card dated 28 June 2018 that I found inside a copy of Olivia Laing's excellent reflection on urban solitude, *The Lonely City* (Canongate), was one of theirs. It just says PRINCIPAL on one side; on the other side it predicts sunshine and a temperature range from 16 to 26 degrees centigrade. In *The Lonely City*, Laing writes about a cape made by her friend Larry: 'It felt nourishing, somehow, a totem object of a kind of collaboration that had not involved actual contact, actual proximity, but that had nonetheless created links, drawing together a community of strangers, scattered through time.'

A collection of second-hand books, especially one that prioritises books containing personal items, or names, addresses, phone numbers, even coffee stirrers, seems to function in a similar way. It feels nourishing.

I email S, whose membership card (expired) for the Audience Club I find inside a copy of Rachel Joyce's *The Love Song of Miss Queenie Hennessy* (Black Swan). My email cannot be delivered. I Google S and the college to which her email address (retired) belongs and find her featured in a college publication from 2014, listed among those members of staff leaving the college that year. For some reason I flip to the previous page and find a photograph of, and write-up for, an old friend of mine who I now remember had taught at the college and has, very sadly, since died. I look up the Audience Club and see that it is a membership organisation that offers free tickets to members for a range of arts events as seat fillers. 'What is the first rule of Secret Seat Filling? We don't talk about seat filling.' Discretion is strongly advised, hence my not revealing S's name.

Even in an example like this, where S no longer works where she worked, meaning I can't contact her to offer to return her card, which obviously she wouldn't want back anyway, and where I'm reminded that a good friend of mine from school days has passed away, there's some comfort to be found in the very small-worldness of the coincidence.

On Saturday 11 November 2023, I'm in Birmingham for a day-long Joel Lane symposium at Voce Books and I get a phone call from an unknown number. It's Suzanne, the niece of the gentleman whose pay slip I found in a copy of *Brideshead Revisited*. Her uncle died seven years ago, his wife more recently. It had fallen to Suzanne to clear the house. There were enough books to open a bookshop, she said. She was kind not to point out that there was one more than there needed to have been.

Later the same month, in Jambala in Bethnal Green, I find a lovely Pan edition of Ian Fleming's *For Your Eyes Only* with an address in King's Avenue, SW4, and a date, 2.9.1963, and a name, J Collins. I stick it through the appropriate door on King's Avenue. No response so far, but that's fine. I don't need a response. If someone opens one of these packages and thinks, 'Oh, that's nice,' and puts the book on a shelf, that's great. If they open it and think, 'WTF,' that's fine, too. No, really, even when I've spent hours at the library scrolling through microfilm to check on an unlikely-sounding name, like Darke Deryk, whose name and address on Smedley Lane in Cheetham Hill, Manchester, had been written in turquoise ink on the inside front cover of a 1966 Panther edition of Maude Hutchins' novel *Honey on the Moon*, which I started reading but didn't get far into before sticking it through the door where it once used to live.

On the Tuesday before Christmas I head down to Tooting on the tube and then walk to Mitcham, where I deliver what was once Canon Graham Smith's copy of *The Jaguar Smile* to his old address on Gorringe Park Avenue. There was one of those little white address labels on the flyleaf. The 'Canon' part was in brackets. The phone number had an 01 prefix, but I didn't need to check when 01 went out of service as the prefix for London (1990) because Canon Smith had also written a note – 'Given to me by Peter Price, May 1987' – and added his signature.

A WhatsApp arrives that evening from Adelina Mason, who lives at Canon Graham Smith's old address with her husband. They have only lived there since 2021 and recently got married. Addy, 29, works for Surrey County Council as an Area Schools Officer. She studied history at Warwick and the opportunity to dig into the past appeals to her. She wonders whether Canon Graham Smith was a priest at All Saints Church in Tooting and subsequently became Dean of Norwich, which seems highly plausible. We both find, online, the opening page of an article from the *Expository Times*, 'This is the Word of the Lord', by Canon Graham Smith.

It occurs to me that I have never found anything – an inclusion, a name, an address – in a copy of the *Bible*. That's hardly surprising, since I just don't tend to go to that part of the bookshop. So I make a special trip on the way back from the dentist and visit all the charity shops in Didsbury Village and don't find a single copy of the *Bible*, apart from a children's bible in Mind, but it's very big and has no distinguishing features. In the Didsbury Village Bookshop I approach the religion section. I look around first to see if there's anyone in I know. There's no one in at all. I'm not being funny – well, I hope I am being funny – but I feel a bit like how I imagine someone might feel as they part the coloured plastic strips to enter the back room of one of those old second-hand book and magazine shops that seem oddly fewer in number now, perhaps because of the internet. There's one paperback *Bible* – nothing of interest – and one absolutely massive *Family Bible* that has 'THE WORD OF GOD' in huge letters on the end papers at the front and £30 pencilled in on the flyleaf.

In Oxfam I spot a shadow line on the top edge of David F Ford's *Theology: A Very Short Introduction* (Oxford). I remove the book and open in to page 11, where there's a blank postcard of a painting by Pieter de Hooch and a small piece of paper about two inches square. Written on it in very beautiful handwriting is this short message: 'Theology is something we can all be engaged in.'

10

Project For a Walk in New York

It is a perfect day in late November: not too cold, clear blue sky, bright low winter sunshine that engulfs you the moment you cross one of the north-south streets that, along with their east-west counterparts, turn this part of the city into a grid. I enter a used record store. While I'm waiting for the man behind the counter to finish serving a customer, I look down at the floor and see a passport-size photograph of a man in late middle age. I pick it up. He has receding grey hair, downturned mouth and jowls. He is unsmiling, as we are required to be in this kind of photograph, but he has recently shaved. He is wearing a navy polo-type shirt with pale blue and white horizontal stripes. There appears to be something underneath this – a vest, another T-shirt, or possibly a lanyard. I want to use my forefinger and thumb to make the photograph bigger – I feel them already trying to enact the manoeuvre – and it's frustrating that I can't.

I look around. The man is not in, but it's likely he has been, recently. I have probably stood next to him at some point, browsing the racks. To be honest, I'm surprised I don't recognise him. If I were to hand the photograph to the man behind the counter, when he has finished with his customer, he would no doubt name the man and take it off me, saying he will give it to him next time he's in. Which is why I don't hand it to him, slipping it instead into the outside breast pocket of my jacket.

'Nicholas,' says the man behind the counter, finished with his customer.

'Rae,' I say.

Rae and I talk for a few minutes, before he asks if I have brought in some items to exchange. I produce them and he evaluates them. I spend five minutes looking in the racks, where some new additions have appeared since my last visit. Normally I pick items to the same value and take them to the counter. On this occasion I take one CD, which is priced at more than I've got to spend, but I know I want this and it might go, and as Rae says to me, it's good to break the rules one sets for oneself. I think he's right. We talk some more before I leave and re-enter the grid of streets. From my jacket pocket I take out a paperback edition of Paul Auster's *The New York Trilogy*, turn to the first page of *City of Glass* and start reading.

The New York Trilogy entered my life in the shape of the first UK edition, published in hardback by Faber & Faber in 1987, jacket illustration by Irene von Treskow, a black and white image of Manhattan superimposed with nineteen individual objects, in colour, most of them red. There are three American flags, two bullets (unless one of them is a lipstick designed to resemble a bullet), a mail box, a postage stamp vending machine, a keep-left sign, a telephone, cup and saucer, exit sign, fire hydrant, ice lolly, ketchup bottle (Heinz), hand-held cut-out letters reading 'WOW', a pointing hand, a red skull, a red ball or possibly an apple, and a detective figure in fedora and trench coat. My copy contains an inclusion at page 231, a gift tag bearing the words

'Happy Christmas Nicholas with love from Mum & Dad xxx'. It's reasonable to assume that this was Christmas 1987, when I was 24. Had I asked for it and if so why? New York took up a considerable amount of space in my imagination and, although in the US I had only been to Boston and Andover, Mass, I felt as if I had also been to New York from the sheer number of films and TV shows I had watched that had been set and, as far as I knew, filmed there. Maybe the specific prompt had been Alain Robbe-Grillet's 1970 novel *Project For a Revolution in New York*, but it could just as easily have been John Carpenter's 1981 film *Escape From New York*. I loved both – and still do.

I read *The New York Trilogy* shortly after being given it for Christmas. I have a snapshot-type memory of reading it on the tube. I can see myself sitting on this side of the carriage, the book out in front of me, but then, it occurs to me, wouldn't one always be sitting on this side, not on that side, of the carriage? The idea that one might be able to see oneself sitting on the other side of the carriage is surely the kind of idea that would not have been out of place in Auster's novel, which is not one novel, but three, if you can count each story as a novel, and one of them is very short. The three parts were published separately in the first instance, in the US, and later combined. In some other territories they were published separately as well, but not in the UK.

Auster himself refers to the three parts of the trilogy as novels in the interview with Larry McCaffery and Sinda Gregory in Auster's 1995 non-fiction work *The Red Notebook*, which is good enough for me.

I read it and loved it.

I read it again at some point in the next ten or fifteen years and still loved it. I decided to reread it for this project, not without some concern that it might have lost its magic for me, that I might have grown out of it. Maybe it's a young person's book or even, quite possibly, a young man's book.

The copy of the novel that I bought from Oxfam Dalston on Thursday 23 November 2023, the 1988 paperback edition with a trimmed-down version of Irene von Treskow's hardback jacket illustration (we lose a few of those iconic images), has a name written in black ink at the top of the flyleaf – S Parham – and an inscription lower down, in gold pen and different handwriting, that reads, 'Hey! Paco! This one's a wild one! Enjoy the ride! James 30/05/13.' James's message reinforces that slight concern that maybe *The New York Trilogy* is a young man's book.

One thing that has happened in the last ten or fifteen years is that I have read Siri Hustvedt's *The Blindfold* – twice, possibly three times. I loved that, too. Siri Hustvedt and Paul Auster are married and live together in Brooklyn, New York. You probably already knew that. It's possible that I love *The Blindfold* more than *The New York Trilogy* – that's one of the things I will find out when I reread *The New York Trilogy* over the coming days – but let's not get into that now. It's a distraction.

I have bought a number of second-hand copies of the trilogy over the last couple of years. I have not been trying to acquire different editions, although that has happened inevitably as part of the process, but copies containing some form of distinguishing mark or intervention, be it an inclusion or an author signature or the name of a former owner. The copy I take out of my pocket as I leave Vinyl Exchange in Manchester's Northern Quarter – I cheated a bit by calling it a used record store when normally I would say second-hand record shop – is the Faber A-format paperback edition dated 1999.

I have two copies of this edition. The one I do not take out of my pocket as I leave Vinyl Exchange (because it's not in my pocket, it's at home) has a bit of the flyleaf torn off, at the bottom, where, I imagine, someone had written a mobile number. I bought that copy on Saturday 13 May 2023 from Oxfam Books & Music Islington.

The cover of this edition is designed by Pentagram, employing a cover photo, credited to John Wilkes, of the Empire State Building. It's a blue, almost turquoise, image with the title in darker-blue foil and Auster's name in red. There are no distinguishing features about this copy, the one I take out of my pocket as I leave Vinyl Exchange. That was deliberate. I bought it from the Global Educational Trust bookshop in Sale on Saturday 10 September 2022. I say 'bought'. In fact, the books in this charity bookshop are free, as long as you take no more than three on any one visit, but there's a money box for donations, should you wish to make one. I had overheard a conversation, in Oxfam Cheadle, about this place in the summer of 2022 and visited it for the first time in July of that year, walking there via Wythenshawe Park and Sale Moor. On that occasion I selected Robert Byron's *The Road to Oxiana*, a Picador I already had but with a different cover, and Leigh Kennedy's *Saint Hiroshima*, because it's a white-spined Abacus paperback with a good cover, and Graham Greene's *Travels With My Aunt*, in a Folio Society edition that I thought I would donate to Oxfam. I left the shop feeling a little uncomfortable, as I didn't have any change, so went back and folded a fiver into the donation box, then walked on to look at the bungalow on Wentworth Drive where as a teenager I used to do gardening for an elderly couple, and then on to have another look at the house on Dorrington Road where I was born. Then I walked back home, reading the manuscript of my PhD student Hazell Ward's experimental crime novel, *Glint of Light*.

I visited the Global Educational Trust bookshop again in

September, picking out a Penguin Modern Classics edition of James Joyce's *Dubliners* with an inclusion at page 84, a Jobseeker's Allowance Information Sheet. Page 84 happens to be the start of the story 'Counterparts', the title I gave to my first novel, which I wrote mostly while on the dole in the late 1980s. Also, a self-published hardback, *Not on the Agenda* (New Horizon) by Nicholas Gilbert, signed by the author to Michael and Mary. 'Choose an author as you choose a friend,' went the dedication. My third book was the paperback edition of *The New York Trilogy*, with, as I say, no distinguishing features, but I decided it would be a reading copy, it would be the copy that I would read as part of my project, a project that I thought at the time might take me back to New York. Wouldn't it be good, I thought, to reread the novel in New York, walking around the streets of Manhattan like Auster's characters? That remained my plan for a while, until I finally accepted that I had run out of time, money and moral justification, in light of the climate crisis, for getting on a plane just to go for a walk.

You may or may not know that Manchester's Northern Quarter often stands in for New York in films. *Captain America: The First Avenger* (2011) was partly filmed there. You can still see evidence of set dressing in the form of scraps of flyposters on windows on Dale Street. In February 2020 I walked through Stevenson Square with US short story writer Sakinah Hofler, who had won the 2017 Manchester Fiction Prize and returned to the city for the prize-giving ceremony for the 2019 prize, for which she was among the judges. We found green street signs, yellow cabs and blue police cars, the streets having been taken over for filming of season four of *The Crown*, featuring Princess Diana's visit to New York.

Manchester, then, will stand in for New York for me. If you

compare the maps, the angle of the streets is almost identical. North-south streets actually run from north-east to south-west, east-west streets, therefore, from south-east to north-west. I walk east (or south-east) along Dale Street as I read the opening pages. 'It was a wrong number that started it, the telephone ringing three times in the dead of night, and the voice on the other end asking for someone he was not.' 'He' is Quinn, who writes mysteries under the pen name William Wilson. He makes no explicit reference at this point to Edgar Allan Poe, whose 'William Wilson' is one of the great doppelgänger stories. Quinn hides behind Wilson, but doesn't feel any great affinity with his pseudonym, being closer to his private-eye narrator, Max Work. The voice on the other end of the phone, however, doesn't ask for Quinn, or for Wilson, or for Work, for that matter, but for Paul Auster of the Auster Detective Agency.

Quinn says there's no one of that name at this number and, after the caller has hung up, regrets not finding out more about 'the case'.

The following night, the telephone rings again and Quinn decides to answer, but he's busy, sitting on the toilet. Should he continue at his normal speed or should he finish quickly? He gets to the phone, but the caller has gone.

Eventually he speaks to the caller again and impersonates Auster. The caller is going to be murdered and wants Auster to protect him, to find the would-be murderer. The caller asks Quinn to come to an address on East 69th Street the following day. 'I'll be there,' says Quinn.

Auster, the real Auster, has spoken of the experience that inspired this opening, in the interview conducted with him by Joseph Mallia, which is also reprinted in *The Red Notebook*. He answered the telephone at home one night to a caller asking for the Pinkerton Detective Agency. The same person rang back the next night and asked the same question. After hanging up, Auster wondered what would have happened if he had answered in the positive.

I walk around the grid of streets enclosed by Newton Street, Dale Street, Oldham Street and Swan Street, still reading, and somewhere near Dale Street I notice a man ahead of me, walking slowly, leaning slightly forwards, stopping every now and then to look up. He's wearing grey trousers, a black jacket and a dark green baseball cap. I cross the street and draw level, the width of the street between us. He is carrying a decent-looking digital SLR camera around his neck and holding on to it with his left hand. He stops to take a picture of some graffiti and I imagine taking a picture of him taking a picture. I get my phone out, but I'm too slow. He's on the move again. Crossing Newton Street I get closer to him. He has grey hair under the cap and a couple of weeks of grey-white beard growth. He's maybe 70, no more than 75. I follow him down Brewer Street. I wonder if he's going to take the footbridge over the canal, but he follows the path around to the right, skirting the car park. I follow him into Piccadilly Station, where I lose him, because I am distracted by the sight of Steve Pemberton and Reece Shearsmith, of *Inside No. 9*, crossing the concourse – Pemberton in front, Shearsmith following – to look at the passenger information display. They will be looking for the next train to London Euston. I watch them turn away from the display, in a hurry now, Pemberton in front once more. He is carrying a wheeled suitcase by its carry handle, not wheeling it, and has a shoulder bag. He is wearing a black puffer jacket. Shearsmith is wearing a short overcoat, white trainers and brown scarf and he, too, is carrying a shoulder bag. I take a photograph of them as they pass the gates to platforms 4 and

5 that I will tweet later: 'Wanted to direct these two gentlemen to platform No. 9, but I see that in a sense they were already there.'

Of course, when I look for my photographer again, he's disappeared. I leave the station and continue walking home, reading. Quinn, as Auster, goes to East 69th Street and meets, first of all, Virginia Stillman, who tells him she is the wife of Peter Stillman, to whom he had spoken on the phone. She takes him in to see Peter, who speaks at great length about what has happened to him in the past and what he fears is on the cards for the future, unless Auster can prevent it happening. Virginia Stillman and Quinn then have a private conversation and on page 31, while she is out of the room looking for a picture of Peter Stillman's father to give to Quinn, Quinn finds himself imagining, not for the first time, what she would look like without any clothes on. Virginia Stillman returns and hands Quinn a photograph of Peter Stillman's father. After looking at it, he slips it into the inside breast pocket of his jacket, where it joins a cheque that Virginia Stillman has already given him that he knows he will not be able to cash, as it is in Auster's name.

As I read this, I remove from the outside breast pocket of my jacket the picture I picked up from the floor of Vinyl Exchange and put it instead into my inside breast pocket.

In this 1999 edition 'cheque' is mostly spelled the British way, but there's one instance of the US spelling, in the first line of the third paragraph on page 31. By the time we get to the 2004 edition, with a cover designed by Two Associates and featuring a greenish monochrome image of what looks like an apartment building, title in white and Auster's name in gold foil, the single instance of US spelling, 'check', has been corrected to 'cheque'. (My page references relate to the 1999 edition, which is the same as the 1987, 1988 and 1992 editions. They will be slightly out for the 2004 and 2011 editions.)

As I walk along Birch Grove, with Birchfields Park on my left, the light is failing. I can hear footsteps some way behind me. I can only really read now in the intermittent pools of light from streetlamps. I want to carry on reading, because I am intrigued by the fact that, as Quinn is taking his leave of Virginia Stillman at the end of chapter three, she throws her arms around him and kisses him passionately. By now there's so little light I have to remove my glasses and hold the book closer to my face. As a result of this faffing about I am walking more slowly, which has allowed the man who had been behind me to overtake me, so that I am then following him, which I continue to do, putting the book back in the pocket of my jacket when the light from the streetlamps is insufficient to read by, the print in this A-format edition being a little on the small side.

I follow the man only because he happens to be going the way I would normally go, which is the reverse of the route I took when Lynne-Anne started talking to me in another chapter, 'Walking and reading', when I was reading *Anacoluthe* by Basile Panurgias. The man ahead of me enters an address on Fairholme Road and I carry on on my own.

Quinn buys himself a red notebook, which is nice, what with Auster publishing a book called *The Red Notebook*. We have referred to it a couple of times. Part one of *The Red Notebook* is also called *The Red Notebook* and is a series of anecdotes, thoughts, memories and short narratives that make up a memoir. Part two is made up of three prefaces, the first of which, on twentieth-century French poetry, might seem a little long if you're not into twentieth-century French poetry. Things pick up a bit with

'Mallarmé's Son' and a lot with 'On the High Wire', about Philippe Petit, the high-wire walker who in 1974 performed a walk between the two towers of the World Trade Center. Parts three, four and five are all essential reading for Auster fans, incorporating the interviews already referred to, 'A Prayer For Salman Rushdie' and finally a piece with the title 'Why Write?'

On page 41 of *The New York Trilogy*, Quinn, his red notebook in his pocket, uses his alumni card to enter the library of Columbia University to do some research on Stillman. One of the interesting elements of this chapter, in which Quinn studies a book written by Stillman, a man with some pretty serious issues if what his son has told Quinn is correct, is the fact that Quinn is able to use his alumni card to gain access to the Columbia library. I've checked and not only could he have done this in the 1980s, but he would still be entitled to do it today. 'Alumni of Columbia University enjoy free lifetime access to library buildings,' according to the university's web site. This seems only fair and reasonable. Does the University of London offer the same entitlement to its alumni, of whom I am one? No, it does not, which is a great pity. As a student, I spent a lot of time in Senate House Library, which bears more than a passing resemblance to the Empire State Building, and I would love to do so again.

Chapter seven finds Quinn at Grand Central Station waiting to spot Stillman and then follow him, but first he sees a young woman reading one of his books. His reaction is complicated, not the 'sudden, unexpected pleasure' he had anticipated, were it ever to happen. He can't tear his eyes away from her. She, on the other hand, isn't impressed. '"You got a problem, mister?"'

He asks her if she likes the book. Bad move. '"I've read better and I've read worse."'

Maybe all writers would like this to happen, until it actually happens. I have never seen a stranger reading one of my books. I have twice been told that someone has seen someone reading one of my books and in each case I was able to work out that the reader was someone I knew.

Their conversation goes on and still he doesn't reveal that he is the author of the book she is reading. 'It's just a book,' she ends up saying. He considers telling her who he is, then decides it makes no difference. He is angry; his pride is hurt. Still, I find the next line surprising. 'Rather than punch the girl in the face, he abruptly stood up from his seat and walked away.' I might be wrong, but I doubt Auster would write that line today.

As a shadow line prospector, there are two things I don't like to find. One is a regular bookmark, whether it's from Daunt Books, Slightly Foxed or Primrose Hill Books, mass-produced or handmade, laminated in plastic, or crocheted, knitted or embroidered, get it away from me.

I love a bus, tram or train ticket. I love a boarding pass. I'm more than happy to find a postcard, business card or Debenhams store card (inside Irène Némirovsky's *Fire in the Blood*, which I found in Mark Jackson-Hancock's extremely well-kept Chapter Two Community Bookshop in Chesham. Mrs M Sussum, get in touch if you'd like it back). I'm over the moon if I find a PR's request for support for a book addressed to a former member of Blur (PG Wodehouse's *Blandings*) or a personal message on hotel memo paper for a founding member of Del Amitri (Anaïs Nin's *Little Birds*).

I love these accidental bookmarks that were perhaps the first thing to hand and reveal something, however minor or insubstantial, about the book's former owner, but I hate a bookmark that says 'Bookmark', whether literally or not. OK, maybe 'hate' is a strong word. But imagine the disappointment. You see the shadow line. You carefully remove the book and maybe you need to flick through or maybe it just falls open at the right page and there it is, a *bookmark*. I mean, why would you buy a bookmark when there are dozens of things within reach that could do the job for free? Why would you spend half an hour making one, when you could spend half an hour writing invective against bookmarks instead?

The other thing is a folded-over page corner. Obviously that's pretty hideous to begin with – who would do that to a book? – but to mistake a folded-over page corner for a genuine shadow line, that's up there with thinking you'd bought Kellogg's Corn Flakes and discovering you've actually brought home a box of Harvest Morn Corn Flakes.

And yet, I see that I have bought two copies of *The New York Trilogy* with folded-over page corners. I found a copy of the 2004 edition in Mind in Dalston in Hackney with a folded-over page corner at page 43, in the middle of Quinn's researching into Stillman in the Columbia library, and a receipt from Oxfam Dalston at page 49. As well as spending 99p on the book, the buyer also spent £4.99 on vinyl. The receipt is dated 23 November 2019. My diary reminds me I was leading a workshop in Macclesfield that day, so it definitely wasn't me. The other copy with a folded-over page corner is the 2011 edition, the cover for which is mostly typographical, with Auster's name embossed in yellow and the title embossed in white, both with spot varnish. If these terms mean nothing to you, don't worry about it. They add verisimilitude but they're not important. Down at the bottom there's an image about two inches by one inch. A row of windows with venetian blinds pulled down. One window has its blind up and there we see a man on the phone. The image is credited to Monalyn Gracia. The folded-over corner is page 53 and it's a big one, bigger than the other one. Page 53 is the scene with Quinn and the young woman reading one of his books. I bought this book from a bookshop that opened up in Withington in Manchester in 2022 and closed down at some point in 2023.

I heard that a guy called Kane Martin was opening a bookshop, in fact a book and record shop, above a café in Withington, which is only a mile up the road from me, so naturally I was very excited. Plus, Kane was friends with a couple of friends of mine. At the time I was trying to find a home for about three decades' worth of *Sight & Sound* magazines that I thought deserved better than the recycling bins. I offered them to Kane and he agreed to take them, on condition that I didn't mind if he used some of them to create a collage-type mural on one of the walls of the shop. Sounds good to me, I said. So he did that and the collage looked great. The rest he offered for sale in the shop along with his records and books. I felt he was overcharging on the books and gently offered my opinion, but Kane said they were his books, as in his own books from his own collection, so I understood he didn't just want to give them away. Still, £6 for *The New York Trilogy*? Even if it was the 2011 edition. In fact, especially seeing as how it was the 2011 edition. With a big folded-over page corner.

I didn't see it when I first went, but the second time I called in, when Kane wasn't there, I saw it on the shelf and even with that £6 pencilled on the flyleaf I knew I had to have it, partly to support Kane and partly for my growing collection of copies of *The New York Trilogy*. I had decided at that point that a folded-over page corner counted as a distinguishing feature. So I stepped up, but I only had either a fiver or a tenner and the young woman didn't have any change and the card machine wasn't working, so I got it for a fiver, still pretty expensive, easily the most I've paid for a copy of *The New York Trilogy*. (My parents paid £10.95 for the first edition in 1987.) Did Kane ever read the whole book or was page 53 as far as he got? I don't know. Nor do I know why the bookshop closed down, but I'd hazard a guess it was because his prices were too high. He was a nice guy, very enthusiastic, with a real passion for music and books (and film). I hope he's thriving.

I have a small handwritten card from Paul Auster dated 28 May 1996. *Dear Mr Royle*, he wrote. *Thank you so much for thinking of me. Ordinarily, I would give it a try – but I'm buried in a book these days and can't think about anything else. Forgive me. And best of luck with the collection. Yours, Paul Auster.*

The book he was writing may have been *Timbuktu*, which was published in 1999. The book I was writing to ask him to contribute to was probably *The Time Out Book of New York Short Stories*, although Auster is not a big short story writer. Maybe I thought, in my naivety, I could coax one out of him. I appreciated him going to the trouble to write back. What a palaver it was in those days. You had to formulate a polite response, find an envelope, root around for a stamp and then head out to the mailbox.

Something very surprising happens on page 56. I won't spoil it for you, in case you haven't read it.

Quinn starts following Stillman, to find out what he's up to and keep him away from Peter. Virginia Stillman has asked him to check in with reports on a daily basis.

Stillman walks around the streets picking things up and either discarding them or putting them in a bag. He has a notebook – a red notebook, like Quinn's, but smaller – in which he stops to write things down, just as Quinn stops to make his own notes about Stillman's activities. I start to wonder how great a difference there is between Stillman's scavenging and my own evolving habits of picking up playing cards, business cards and security cards; notes, photographs and shopping lists.

Quinn starts to worry that when he stops to make a note about Stillman, he might lose sight of him, so he experiments, but finds that 'walking and writing were not easily compatible activities'. I can confirm this. 'Finally, he decided to rest the notebook on his left hip, much as an artist holds his palette.' I've tried that; results are not encouraging.

I've skimmed over one or two more tiny errors, partly because it seems pointless to highlight tiny errors in a masterpiece, because it is a masterpiece, or at least that's what I'm thinking at this point. Any concerns that I had that it would not be as good as I remembered have melted away. There's an apostrophe missing on page 48, a 'discrete' on page 60 that should be 'discreet', and a mark on page 78 that looks like a rogue full stop. On page 108 there are 'saxaphonists', on page 124 'skiis'. Letter spaces are missing on pages 128 and 291. On page 305, we read 'in the mean time'. All of these are corrected in the 2004 edition, which brings me to the point I would make. I find it heartening that so much trouble has been gone to, in order to end up with something close to perfection.

Diamonds are classified according to how many inclusions or blemishes are visible under 10x magnification. The best grade is known as flawless. It's possible *The New York Trilogy* may now be flawless.

Having said which, I place great value on copies that contain my kind of inclusions. Or, to be precise, I like to go out and find copies that contain inclusions. If you were to send me one, that would be kind, but it would not be the same. Just as the person who stands on the rocks casting a lure into the ocean in the hope of catching a pollock, for example, does not want to be handed one by somebody walking by.

On Tuesday 12 April 2022 I took the train to Forest Hill, south London, intending to check out a second-hand book and record shop, Leaf & Groove, which my wife had visited with friends. It turned out it was only open Fridays, Saturdays and Sundays, so I walked to Crystal Palace and then on to West Norwood where I found Celia Fremlin's first novel, *The Hours Before Dawn*, in the Emmaus charity shop. My destination was the excellent Book & Record Bar run by the charming and well-connected Michael Johnson. I don't know if I've been lucky or if all visitors here are offered a coffee once they have started browsing. I also don't know if it's a coincidence that Michael Johnson's personal Twitter handle contains the letters 'orb' and in his shop on another occasion he pointed out to me Alex Paterson from The Orb, who had just finished a DJ set.

The next time I went to Forest Hill to try to visit Leaf & Groove, I found it had closed down just days earlier. One to add to the list of the ones that got away.

Back to 12 April 2022, possibly the only day on which I have found two interesting copies of *The New York Trilogy* in the same shop on the same day. In fact, to own up, I had seen one of them before – the one in which a previous reader has written on the flyleaf the words 'Unreliable narrator' – and not thought it worth buying. Almost as soon as I had left the shop on that occasion, I knew I ought to have bought it, hence my going back, and on this return trip, I found not only that copy still on the shelf, but also another copy of the same edition, the 2004 edition, in the basement, containing numerous inclusions.

The first one is at page 87, by which point Quinn has lost Stillman. He has, in the meantime, approached him and had conversations with him, and now he has lost him and so enters the hotel where Stillman has been staying to ask for him, but the man in the hotel is not helpful. At page 87, then, is a torn-off part of a box that once contained a 30g tube of Betamethasone valerate cream, a topical corticosteroid. At later points in the book we find two receipts, one from Oxfam Bookshop Herne Hill, where the previous owner seems to have bought the book (along with two others) in 2015, and one from OHSO Social Beach Bar & Restaurant, Brighton, dated September 2009; a business card for a NatWest bank manager, St Paul's branch; and a feedback card from OHSO Social with a corner torn off and an 01983 phone number written in the comments box. I called the number and got a familiar message: 'The number you have dialled has not been recognised.'

Another receipt in another copy of the same edition. This one is from B&Q in Nottingham, the receipt, that is, where, on 17 May 2007, the book's owner spent £29.44 on paint. The receipt is at page 91, the first page of chapter ten, which begins, 'Stillman was gone now.' I found this copy in the Global Educational Trust bookshop in Sale on Thursday 27 April 2023. And another receipt, inside another copy of the same edition, which I bought from Oxfam Bookshop Chorlton on Thursday 13 July 2023. The receipt, which comes ten pages into *Ghosts*, is for £20 spent on Paypoint in the Coop. On the back of the receipt is a mobile number with an 07835 prefix, which I texted a couple of times, failing to get a response.

I try emailing Zinaran, Jason and Michelle, whose email addresses I find written on the inside back cover of another copy of the 2004 edition that I find in Crisis in Dalston on Tuesday

31 October 2023. No responses. There's also a web address that is currently 'parked'.

In chapter ten, Quinn goes to visit Auster, hoping to find the man who runs the Auster Detective Agency, but finding instead Paul Auster, the writer, who invites him in, listens to his story and offers to make him a ham omelette. They talk about *Don Quixote*, which Auster is writing about, and then Auster's wife, Siri, turns up.

As James wrote to Paco in 2013, 'This one's a wild one!' But my fears that it might, to this middle-aged man, feel like a young man's book have proved unfounded. It's also a novel that seems to speak directly to women despite the fact that most of the main characters are men. In *The Lonely City*, Olivia Laing writes about going to live in New York. 'Almost as soon as I arrived, I was aware of a gathering anxiety around the question of visibility. I wanted to be seen, taken in and accepted, the way one is by a lover's approving gaze. At the same time I felt dangerously exposed, wary of judgment, particularly in situations where being alone felt awkward or wrong, where I was surrounded by couples or groups. While these feelings were undoubtedly heightened by the fact that I was living in New York for the first time – that city of glass, of roving eyes – they arose out of loneliness, which agitates always in two directions, towards intimacy and away from threat.'

Writer and artist Andrea Mason, an accomplished author of list stories, sends me a list of things she loves about *The New York Trilogy* that picks up the theme of isolation explored by Laing: 'Unknowable protagonists; an author-namesake-character; hostile technology; labyrinthine Kafkaesque plot lines; amplified isolation.'

My search for inclusions, for names of former owners, for phone numbers and email addresses, is not only a fishing expedition but also a reaching-out. I want to find a name that means something to me, whether it's someone I know, or someone who knows someone I know, or someone famous, or whatever. So, when, on Monday 9 January 2023, in Jambala charity bookshop in Bethnal Green, I found a copy of the 1988 edition with, in black ink on the flyleaf, the name Danny Boyle, I was pretty excited. A quick Google confirmed it as Boyle's signature. I wonder why none of the three novels that make up the trilogy have ever been filmed. Did Boyle read it for professional reasons, I wonder, or for pleasure?

Auster wrote and (with Wayne Wang) co-directed *Smoke* (1995), starring William Hurt, Harvey Keitel, Stockard Channing and Forest Whitaker. It received a screening at the BFI, in NFT1, on Saturday 6 October 2012, in the presence of Auster. In the audience was Julia, from London, who had ordered a copy of *The New York Trilogy* from Amazon in September the previous year. She took it along to the screening of *Smoke* in 2012 and got it signed by the author. He signed with a black Sharpie, Julia's name in caps, his signature recognisable from the card he had sent me in 1996. Somehow the book ended up in Oxfam Books & Music Kentish Town, where I bought it on Saturday 8 January 2022.

'Auster's flukes and chance events are, effectively, a philosophical comment on the randomness of life,' writes novelist Kerry Hadley-Pryce to me in an email when I discover that she, too, is a fan. 'Coincidence, for him,' she adds, 'is a narrative element.'

For Quinn, things get worse before they get better – if they get better at all. There's something about the ending of *City of Glass* that reminds me, in a good way, of Stanley Kubrick's *2001: A Space Odyssey* (1968).

There's something about Quentin Tarantino's *Reservoir Dogs* (1992) that reminds me, not in a good way, of *Ghosts*, the second novel in *The New York Trilogy*. I loved *Reservoir Dogs* when it came out, but seeing it again recently I liked it less. Maybe it's a young man's film?

On Saturday 21 January 2023, in Oxfam Dalston, I found a copy of *The New York Trilogy* containing a postcard, blank on the reverse, of a painting by Ingres, *Comtesse d'Haussonville*, belonging to the Frick Collection. It's at the title page of *Ghosts*.

Ghosts begins: 'First of all there is Blue. Later there is White, and then there is Black, and before the beginning there is Brown. Brown broke him in, Brown taught him the ropes, and when Brown grew old, Blue took over. That is how it begins. The place is New York, the time is the present, and neither one will ever change. Blue goes to his office every day and sits at his desk, waiting for something to happen. For a long time nothing does, and then a man named White walks through the door, and that is how it begins.'

Are you in? Do you see the connection with *Reservoir Dogs*? Beyond the colours-for-names there is no connection. But Auster did it first. Maybe someone did it before Auster? I don't know.

White wants Blue to watch Black. To follow him if he goes out. It's a tail job. White has rented an apartment for Blue across the street from Black's. Blue tells his fiancée he's going under cover. It will take a while.

So, Blue watches Black. All Black is doing is read. To see the title of the book Black is reading, Blue has to look through binoculars. It reminds me of pausing the DVD to see what books characters are reading in films, advancing frame by frame to get the best angle. Black is reading *Walden* by Henry David Thoreau. It's not the most exciting job Blue has ever had. When Black goes out, Blue follows him. Fortunately, Blue has always been 'an ardent walker'. I, too, am an ardent walker. I can also definitely see the attraction of watching someone in the apartment across the street, even writing a regular report, and following them when they go out. For me, these activities, whether real or imaginary, are closely linked to writing, whether to the writing of the 'Books in films' chapter in this book or to the writing of fiction. When Blue sits in a restaurant watching Black have a meal in the company of a woman, it's almost like we are sitting in the restaurant alongside Blue, or instead of Blue. It's like Blue doesn't exist and we are Blue. When Blue follows Black out of the restaurant on to the street, the act of following, or the description of the act of following, reads like pure narrative, like the creation of fiction.

Blue and Black meet and talk about ghosts.

The names written in the front of some of my copies of *The New York Trilogy* are like ghosts. There's Gillett, for example, whose copy I find in Oxfam Bookshop Bloomsbury Street on 19 March 2023 shortly after my near-miss in Canon Aly, as described in another chapter, 'Walking and reading'. I know nothing about Gillett apart from the fact that he or she owned and probably read *The New York Trilogy* and may have donated it to Oxfam Bookshop Bloomsbury Street, although that book could have had other owners between Gillett and me. I'll never know.

There's William Stanton, whose copy I bought from George Street Books in Glossop on Monday 16 October 2023, the day I met Amanda Huggins (by arrangement), Joanne from Batley (by chance) and Sophie Pattinson (in George Street Books). William

Stanton had got himself an embossing stamp; on the flyleaf is a lovely, discreet embossed stamp that reads, 'LIBRARY OF WILLIAM STANTON'.

There's Ian Green, who adds the year, 1994, under his name. On Monday 13 November 2023, I dropped into Oxfam Whitworth Park, Manchester, and made a happy discovery – a whole row of Austers – *The Invention of Solitude, In the Country of Last Things, Leviathan, Moon Palace, The Music of Chance* and *The New York Trilogy*. The latter was the only one that contained a name. Not only that, but on the inside back cover was another name, David, and a phone number with an 0222 prefix. This would have been a Cardiff number. In 2000, all Cardiff numbers had 20 added to them at the front and a new prefix, 029, before that, so I called 029 20, followed by the rest of the number, but got the message, 'The number you have called is not recognised. Please check the number. If you need help, call the operator on 100 from your mobile.' Well, I probably do need help, but I'm not sure the operator can provide it. I'm looking for a David in the city of Cardiff, last thought to be there in 1994.

There is one tiny spelling error in *Ghosts*.

I found a German edition of the trilogy in Oxfam Bookshop Herne Hill on Friday 21 April 2023. *Die New York-Trilogie* is translated by Joachim A Frank and this edition was published by Rowohlt in 2002. At page 229, six pages from the end of *Ghosts*, is a postcard, blank on the reverse, of *Fat Car* by Erwin Wurm, an Austrian artist whose father was a detective.

Halloween 2022. I walked down Kingsland High Road and called in at St Vincent's where I spent £1 on William Boyd's *Visions Fugitives* (The Cuckoo Press). Then on down to London Bridge. Old Kent Road. Through Burgess Park to Peckham and a Royle Mail delivery. Royle Mail is a joke that works only within the UK. Royal Mail, on the other hand, is a joke that works all over the world. It's not entirely their fault, of course. The government that privatised it can take some of the credit and anyone who voted for Brexit can claim the rest. In Peckham, Nightjar author Cliff McNish seemed pleased to see me. We went out for coffee in East Dulwich. For some reason we talked about Christopher Fowler and his novel *Spanky*. At the café, Cliff's osteopath stopped by our table and I heard myself telling him about my shoulder. A bit later, walking to Herne Hill, reading Andrew Hook's short story collection *Candescent Blooms*, I passed a man who looked so much like Christopher Fowler I almost said hello to him. Then I looked back down at my book and read the name *Spanky*.

In Herne Hill Oxfam Bookshop I found a copy of the 2011 edition of *The New York Trilogy* with a folded-over corner at page 201. In this edition, page 201 is the first page of the third novel, *The Locked Room*.

The Locked Room is narrated in the first person and the narrator is not given a name. *The Locked Room* joins a rich tradition of first-person narratives in which the narrator is not the main character, but someone who enjoys – or enjoyed – privileged access to that character, who tends to be a charismatic figure often draped in a cloak of mystery. There must be dozens of examples of such stories. The one I return to most often is Alain-Fournier's *Le Grand Meaulnes*. In *The Locked Room*, Fanshawe creates his own mystery by vanishing from his life, leaving a wife and baby – and two suitcases full of unpublished writings. The job Fanshawe's wife, Sophie, asks the narrator to take on, rather than to look for Fanshawe, is to read the work and assess it.

I am reading chapter two of *The Locked Room* while walking between Chorlton and Didsbury in south Manchester. The narrator is reminiscing about Fanshawe, his best friend when they were boys. As I approach the bottom of page 219, the narrator is remembering Fanshawe's father nearing the end of his life and I am entering Southern Cemetery. 'There is only one more thing I want to mention here,' writes the narrator as he goes on to recount an episode where he and Fanshawe went for a drive after school. It begins snowing and they enter a cemetery, stopping the car to have a wander. I walk along the avenue that will eventually lead to my dad's grave. They read the inscriptions on the gravestones, as I always do if I'm not already reading a book. As I reach my dad's grave, Fanshawe and the narrator come upon a freshly dug grave. A couple of months ago, there was a freshly dug grave two plots along from my dad's grave. I spent quite a bit of time looking down into it, thinking about climbing down into the grave and lying on my back, looking up at the sky. Fanshawe does exactly that. The narrator helps him climb down into the grave and then watches as the snow falls on Fanshawe's face. 'I understood that this was Fanshawe's way of imagining his father's death,' writes the narrator. 'Again, it was a matter of pure chance: the open grave was there, and Fanshawe had felt it calling out to him.' The next line, in the copy of the 2011 edition of *The New York Trilogy* that I bought from Oxfam Bookshop Cheltenham on Tuesday 14 June 2022, has a black mark by it in the margin. The copy was previously owned by Wolverhampton-based artist Mike Massingham, who had written 'M Massingham. Bilston 2017' in black rollerball on the inside front cover. He also highlighted in orange a number of titles in Auster's author biog. Maybe he had read these, or intended to read them. On the inside back cover are five page references, one of them, with the comment 'Interesting!', to this line on his page 222 (page 221 in the 1999 edition that I am reading): 'Stories happen only to those who are able to tell them, someone once said.' Is this true? It would appear to confer some special status on authors. Even the narrator takes care to distance himself from it by adding 'someone once said'.

Perhaps this is a good point at which to briefly mention another copy of the 2011 edition, which I found in Jambala charity bookshop in Bethnal Green on Wednesday 13 July 2022, with a date on the flyleaf – 6 August 2020 – and a name, Prudence Graves.

As he prepares to read Fanshawe's work, the narrator is conflicted. 'If I did not want Fanshawe's work to be bad, I discovered, I also did not want it to be good.' I think this might be a more common feeling among writers, in specific circumstances, than is publicly acknowledged.

The narrator reads Fanshawe's work and realises it is not just publishable, but of major importance. It will be a publishing sensation. He and Sophie meet for dinner to talk about next steps, but they find there is more going on between them than planning what to do with Fanshawe's work.

Things progress. The narrator publishes an article about Fanshawe. Most nights now the narrator spends with Sophie at her apartment. Then, out of the blue, as it were, a letter arrives. As if to mark this dramatic turning point in the narrative, I find an inclusion, in a copy of the 2004 edition that I buy from the Amnesty Bookshop in Hammersmith on Wednesday 29 November 2023, an Ineuropa Handling boarding pass, no name, no date.

The next line that Mike Massingham marks in his copy (of his 2011 edition) is this one, on page 249, 'We all want to be told stories, and we listen to them in the same way we did when we were young.' I can't disagree with that. I like that bridging of the gap between youth and whatever age we are now. I feel I have answered the question I set out to answer. Would I be less impressed by *The New York Trilogy* now, at this point in my life, than when I first read it at the age of 24? In fact, I am more impressed by it. It turns my head inside out. I love it, probably the same amount as I love Siri Hustvedt's *The Blindfold*, which now I feel I need to reread. *The New York Trilogy* is richer and subtler than I realised as a young man. There are more facets to it than my untrained eyes were able to appreciate. Also in that line I like the specificity of 'listen' – 'we listen to them' – because one thing I have started doing, not with every book I read, but with some, including this one, and I think it has to do with the effect I noticed in the Doris Lessing story, 'An Old Woman and Her Cat', that as I feel I am approaching the end of a story, I become more susceptible to an emotional reaction, is reading the last page, or couple of pages, or just the last paragraph, out loud. So if you were in Manchester's Northern Quarter one after-noon in early January 2024 and you saw a dashingly handsome middle-aged man with his nose in a book talking to himself, now you know why.

I celebrated finishing by trying to call Odette, since texting hadn't worked. Odette's name and number are written on the inside back cover of the Livre de Poche edition of *La chambre dérobée* (*Trilogie new-yorkaise, 3*) that I bought in Mona Lisait in Paris on Sunday 9 July 2023. Sadly, the only response I get is now a familiar one, 'The number you have called is not recognised. Please check the number. If you need help, call the operator on

100 from your mobile.' Earlier in 2023, on 21 March, I found a combined volume, *Trilogie new-yorkaise* (Babel), in the same bookshop, probably my favourite second-hand bookshop in Paris, on rue du Faubourg Saint-Antoine in the 11th. The book's former owner, Marie Thé, had written her name on the flyleaf.

For such a popular book, with what feels like a very strong cult following, it's surprising how few copies I've found with gift inscriptions. Only two, in fact. One came from Oxfam Bookshop Chorlton, on Wednesday 2 February 2022, and I have a slightly bad feeling about it. 'To a very special Dad, lots of love Billie,' the messages begin, and, 'We missed you very much Dad, Pen x, 16.2.91' and finally, 'Love from Lowell.' And the other is the 1992 edition with a cover design by Pentagram featuring Keith Goldstein's photograph of the Statue of Liberty viewed through a series of spot-varnished black slats. I found it in Crisis in Dalston on Tuesday 2 August 2022. The inscription is on the title page – I nearly missed it – and it reads, 'Merry Christmas! Love Kate.'

Acknowledgements

I would like to thank staff and regulars at Mary & Archie and Lapwing Deli in West Didsbury, Manchester, and Belle Epoque, in Islington, London, where large parts of this book were written. I would also like to thank all of the following: Matthew Adamson, John Ashbrook, Penny Ashbrook, Iphgenia Baal, Elizabeth Baines, David Batt, Melanie Boycott, Charles Boyle, Gary Budden, Michael Caines, Richard Clegg, Jonathan Coe, David Collard, Sarah-Clare Conlon, Rafe Conn, Ailsa Cox, Geoff Cox, Laura Cumming, Gary Day-Ellison, Rae Donaldson, Emmanuelle Donnard, Simon Donoghue, Gareth Evans, Iris Feindt, Dell Fielding, Samuel Fisher, David Gaffney, Wayne Gooderham, Nancy Graham, Robert Graham, Kerry Hadley-Pryce, Naomi Hamill, Chris Hamilton-Emery, Jen Hamilton-Emery, Rhodri Hayward, Hilaire, Roger Huss, Andy Jackson, Mick Jackson, Patrick Janson-Smith, Michael Johnson, Clive Judd, Nigel Kendall, Paul Leith, Richard Little, Fraser McIlwraith, Rachel McIntyre, Lucie McKnight Hardy, Cliff McNish, Kane Martin, Adelina Mason, Andrea Mason, Tim Meaker, Livi Michael, Michael Middleton, More Maniacs & everyone at Moniack Mhor, Sonya Moor, Adam Morris, Martin

Needham, Mike Nelson, Craig Nichols-Young, Emma Oakey, John Oakey, Simon Okotie, Sophie Pattinson, Chris Pearson, Janet Penny, Mike Petty, Juliet Pickering, Brian Radcliffe, Cécile Radcliffe, Andrew Ratcliffe, Nick Rogers, David Rose, Bella Royle, Charlie Royle, Jean Royle, Joanna Royle, Julie Royle, Nicholas Royle, Kate Ryan, John Saddler, Ginny Sales, Tim Shearer, Harry Sherriff, John Shire, Adrian Slatcher, Stephen Smith, Yuka Sonobe, Robert Stone, Joe Stretch, Louise Theodosiou, Matthew Thomas, Trevor Mark Thomas, Emma Townshend, Tim Watson, Helen White, Chris Witty, Conrad Williams, Jason Wood. Special thanks to my wife, Ros Sales, and apologies to those people I am bound to have forgotten.

Picadors, published between 1972 and 2001, added to main collection since list in *White Spines*

Russell Banks, *The Sweet Hereafter*

T Coraghessan Boyle, *World's End*

William Burroughs Junior, *Kentucky Ham*

Michael Bywater, *The Chronicles of Bargepole*

Karel Capek, *War With the Newts*

Amit Chaudhuri (ed), *The Picador Book of Modern Indian Literature*

Salvador Dali, *Diary of a Genius*

Luciano De Crescenzo, *Thus Spake Bellavista*

Marquis de Sade, *The Gothic Tales of the Marquis de Sade*

Robert Drewe, *The Bay of Contented Men*

Andre Dubus, *Meditatations From a Movable Chair*

Robert Edric, *The Earth Made of Glass* • *In the Days of the American Museum*

Carlos Fuentes, *The Campaign* • *Myself With Others*
Kate Grenville, *Dark Places*
Cynthia Heimel, *If You Leave Me, Can I Come Too?*
Alice Hoffman, *White Horses*
Tama Janowitz, *American Dad*
Charles Johnson, *Middle Passage*
Ryszard Kapuscinski, *The Emperor/Shah of Shas*
Jonathan Keates, *Italian Journeys*
William Kennedy, *Quinn's Book*
Tracy Kidder, *Among Schoolchildren*
Richard Klein, *Cigarettes Are Sublime* • *Eat Fat*
Arthur Koestler, *The Thirteenth Tribe*
Christopher Lasch, *The Minimal Self: Psychic Survival in Troubled Times*
Norman Lewis, *The Happy Ant Heap*
Barry Lopez, *Arctic Dreams*
Dennis McFarland, *The Music Room*
William McGowan, *Only Man is Vile: The Tragedy of Sri Lanka*
William McGuire (ed) & Alan McGlashan (abridged), *The Freud/Jung Letters*
Joseph O'Connor, *Sweet Liberty: Travels in Irish America*
PJ O'Rourke, *All the Trouble in the World*
Emily Perkins, *Not Her Real Name*
David Profumo, *The Weather in Iceland*
Tony Parker, *The People of Providence*
Joe Queenan, *Imperial Caddy: The Rise of Dan Quayle in America and the Decline and Fall of Practically Everything Else*
Israel Rosenfield, *The Strange, Familiar and Forgotten: An Anatomy of Consciousness*
Ajay Sahgal, *Pool*
Stacy Schiff, *Véra (Mrs Vladimir Nabokov)*

Gilbert Sorrentino, *Mulligan Stew*
Junichiro Tanizaki, *Some Prefer Nettles/The Secret History of the Lord of Musashi/Arrowroot*
John Edgar Wideman, *Brothers and Keepers*
Robert McLiam Wilson & Donovan Wylie, *The Dispossessed*
Theodore Zeldin, *Happiness*

Picador Classics, published 1980s/90s, added to collection since list in *White Spines*

James Agee, *A Death in the Family*
M Ageyev, *Novel With Cocaine*
Sherwood Anderson, *Winesburg, Ohio*
Charles Baudelaire, *Intimate Journals*
Mikhail Bulgakov, *Heart of a Dog* • *The Master and Margarita*
Joseph Conrad, *Lord Jim*
William Faulkner, *Intruder in the Dust* • *The Sound and the Fury*
Haniel Long, *The Marvellous Adventure of Cabeza de Vaca*
Robert Musil, *The Man Without Qualities Volume One* • *The Man Without Qualities Volume Two* • *Tonka & Other Stories*
Rainer Maria Rilke, *The Notebooks of Malte Laurids Brigge*
Joseph Roth, *Hotel Savoy*
John Steinbeck, *The Grapes of Wrath*
Nathanael West, *Complete Works*

This book has been typeset by
SALT PUBLISHING LIMITED
using Granjon, a font designed by George W. Jones
for the British branch of the Linotype company in the
United Kingdom. It is manufactured using Creamy 70gsm,
a Forest Stewardship Council™ certified paper from Stora
Enso's Anjala Mill in Finland. It was printed and bound
by Clays Limited in Bungay, Suffolk, Great Britain.

CROMER
GREAT BRITAIN
MMXXIV